WIVES
OF THE CANADIAN
PRIME MINISTERS

WIVES
OF THE CANADIAN
PRIME MINISTERS

CAROL McLEOD

LANCELOT PRESS
Hantsport, Nova Scotia

ISBN 0-88999-290-8

Published 1985

LANCELOT PRESS LIMITED, Hantsport, N.S.
Office and plant situated on Highway No. 1, ½ mile east of Hantsport

4

To
Anthony Legere,
remembering the days at A.R.H.S.

Photographic credits

CONTENTS

FOREWORD

Of Canada's eighteen prime ministers, only two — Mackenzie King and R.B. Bennett — have been bachelors. The wives of the other sixteen have had the unpaid, repetitious and often thankless job of cutting ribbons, turning sods, unveiling plaques and christening ships. Obviously, there is more to these women than the plastic smiles they have flashed in public. Each has had her own strengths, her own weaknesses; and each has coped in her own way with the strain of public life. Some have been content to live in their husbands' shadows. Others have striven to establish their own identities. All, in some measure, have sacrificed themselves for the advancement of their husbands' careers.

Researching this book and studying the lives of these sixteen women has been an exciting and rewarding experience. Unfortunately, history has not treated them all equally. While some — such as Agnes Macdonald and Annie Thompson — have had their personal papers preserved, others — such as Mary Abbott and Harriet Bowell — remain virtual enigmas. Rather than omit profiles of the women whose lives have been less well documented, I have worked with the information currently available through the Public Archives of Canada.

August, 1985   Carol McLeod

ACKNOWLEDGEMENTS

A great many people have helped gather the reference material used in the preparation of this book. In particular, I should like to thank Lillian Meighen Wright, Don Wright, and Michael Meighen for their recollections and assistance. 1 am also indebted to Marilyn Colpitts, Gwynne Hughes, Dianne Oldham, and Thérèse Arseneault of the Albert-Westmorland-Kent Regional Library; to Franceen Gaudet, Huguette Lussier Tremblay, and Wendy Scott of the National Library of Canada; to Diane Chevrier and Elizabeth Krug of the National Photography Collection, Public Archives of Canada; and to Ian McClymont of the Prime Ministers' Archives, Public Archives of Canada.

For other help too varied to specify I wish to thank Betty Belford, Administrative Assistant, Office of the Prime Minister; Dennis Cochrane, M.P., the staff of his constituency office, and his assistant in Ottawa, Tom Hart; Ernest Coates of Amherst, N.S.; Laddie Farquhar of Halifax, N.S.; Catrona Dalley Galt, Personal Secretary to the Leader, Office of the Leader of the Opposition; the Hastings County Historical Society, Belleville, Ont.; Sandra M. Haycock, Public Records Archivist, Public Archives of Nova Scotia; Alex Pincombe of Moncton, N.B.; Steve Proulx, Librarian, *The Ottawa Citizen*; and Shirley C. Spragge, Assistant Archivist, Queen's University Archives.

Gratitude is also due my aunt, Doris Charman of Halifax, N.S., and to my friend and mentor, Anthony Legere of Amherst, N.S., for the time they devoted to tracking down information on Frances Tupper; to William Pope for his faith and interest in the project; and above all to my husband whose suggestions, criticism, encouragement and support have made all the difference.

AGNES MACDONALD

When the Dominion of Canada officially came into being on July 1, 1867, Agnes Macdonald was a glowing bride just back from an extended visit to England. Celebrations, which had begun in Ottawa on the evening of June 30 to mark the birth of the new nation, had wound her to fever pitch and she was up early on the morning of July 1 to help her husband prepare for the ceremony that would see him installed as the first prime minister of Canada.

She herself had no firm plans for the day: women were not being admitted to the official swearing in and she would be unable to share with John in his moment of glory. Yet any disappointment she may have felt at being excluded from the festivities was short-lived. Before noon a note arrived from her husband addressing her for the first time as Lady Macdonald and explaining that he had just been made a Knight Commander of the Most Honourable Order of the Bath.

Four days later Agnes, unable to contain her joy, started a new diary. "Now I am a great Premier's wife," she wrote, "and Lady Macdonald and 'Cabinet secrets and mysteries' might drop off . . . my pen . . . if I knew any . . . which I certainly don't . . ."

She also confided to her diary that although she enjoyed the novelty of her husband's title and felt it excused her being bumptious for a few days, she did not appreciate the political atmosphere that permeated their home. "Sometimes," she wrote wryly, "I think the very flies hold Parliament on the kitchen tablecloths!"

Agnes Macdonald

Certainly nothing in her formative years had prepared Agnes for the demands of her new life. Born in Jamaica on August 24, 1836, she spent her early childhood on her parents' 500-acre plantation near Spanish Town. By the time she could walk, her father, Thomas Bernard, a member of the Privy Council of Jamaica, had begun to experience financial problems, and in 1840 he gave up his estate and moved his family to Spanish Town. To compensate Agnes and her four brothers for living in the crowded city, Thomas and his wife, Theodora, rented a house each summer in Jamaica's Blue Mountains. In 1845 Agnes wrote a letter to her brother, Hewitt, who was attending school in England telling him of their vacation.

My dear Hewitt

. . . it is very cool up here, we are much more comfortable than we were last year, there is more furniture. Mama and I sit in the little back room. I led in my lessons, the boys do theirs with Papa in the Piazza. . . I have a little garden by the steps, I dig with the small hoe you sent up.

Your affectionate sister

Susan Agnes Bernard

Lessons and gardening were not the only duties that took up Agnes's time. Theodora saw to it that her children received intensive religious instruction, and Agnes — with occasional reluctance — studied her catechism daily.

Within a few years she had outgrown lessons at home and was enrolled at school in Spanish Town. Then, in 1850, an epidemic of Asiatic cholera struck the island and Thomas Bernard died, leaving his son, Hewitt, to take charge of the family. The following year Theodora took Agnes back to England, and after enjoying the wonders of the Great Exhibition in London, the two went to live with relatives in Lacock, near Bath.

Agnes resumed her schoolwork and took up singing, drawing and the study of French. Although her vocal abilities were nominal, she showed a definite flair for drawing and easily mastered French.

13

In 1854 Hewitt, who had established a law practice in Barrie, Ontario, wrote to his mother and sister inviting them to join him in Canada. They accepted and, after landing at Quebec City, travelled to Toronto where Hewitt met them and took them on to Barrie.

While Agnes and Theodora were establishing new lives for themselves in Canada, a 39-year-old lawyer by the name of John Alexander Macdonald was making his voice heard with increasing force in the country's political circles. His first wife, Isabella Clark, had spent much of their 14-year marriage bedridden by a strange and recurring illness, and her death in 1857 had left Macdonald with a seven year old son, Hugh John, and a debilitating fondness for alcohol.

When Agnes first saw the up-and-coming politician at a concert in Toronto in 1858, she felt that his face possessed an intriguing mixture of strengh and vivacity. Although she was not introduced to him at the time, she soon began to hear a great deal about his life and work. Hewitt, who had become involved in a number of newspapers, had written articles that impressed Macdonald, and in 1857 he accepted an offer to move to Toronto and serve as Macdonald's private secretary.

Hewitt's decision meant another uprooting for Agnes and Theodora. Once settled in their new home, however, Agnes began to take an interest in Canadian politics. She went to the House several times and in July, 1858, saw Macdonald, by then head of the Liberal-Conservative Party, debate the issue of selecting a capital city for Canada.

Finally, in the winter of 1860, she met Macdonald for the first time. As a courtesy to Hewitt, Macdonald called on Theodora and Agnes, told them of Hewitt's work and said that he would like to get to know the family. As it turned out, Macdonald had seen Agnes without her knowledge in a restaurant in 1856. When he had asked his companion who the tall woman with the fine eyes was, he had been told that she was a member of an English family recently settled near Lake Simcoe. Her name was not mentioned, and it was not until 1860 that Macdonald realized the woman was his secretary's sister.

It is possible, but not certain, that Macdonald and Agnes developed a friendship during this period. Ever since the death of his first wife, Macdonald had been known as a lady's man, and although Agnes was not beautiful (her broad forehead, heavy eyebrows, aquiline nose, and stern mouth made her somewhat forbidding), her intelligence and piquant charm must certainly have attracted Macdonald's attention.

Whatever the case, in 1865 Agnes and her mother returned to England for an extended visit. The following year a meeting was held in London to discuss plans for Canadian Confederation and one afternoon in mid-December as Macdonald, chairman of the conference, was walking down Bond Street he met Agnes and Theodora. Within weeks Macdonald, twenty-one years Agnes' senior, had proposed and Agnes had accepted.

Macdonald, who had seen his first marriage lived in the shadow of the sickroom, was anxious for the wedding to take place as soon as possible. After settling upon a date in mid-February, he reserved St. George's Church, Hanover Square, and ordered the invitations. Agnes selected a gown of white satin and set about choosing her bridesmaids. One, Emma Tupper, was the daughter of the future Canadian prime minister, Sir Charles Tupper, who was also attending the pre-Confederation Conference.

Finally, on the morning of Saturday, February 16, 1867, Agnes arrived at the church with her brother, Hewitt. After the ceremony a reception for ninety guests was held at the Westminster Palace Hotel. No expense was spared and on each plate lay a nosegay of violets and snowdrops. There was one toast — to Agnes's health — and by late afternoon the bride and groom were on their way to Oxford for a three-day honeymoon.

When business recalled them to London on Tuesday, Agnes hardly had enough time to take off her gloves before she was swept into the whirl of the political circle. The excitement thrilled her, and her presentation to Queen Victoria at Buckingham Palace marked the full measure of her social standing.

In May the Canadian delegation returned home, and Agnes took up her new life in John's former bachelor quarters in Ottawa. With Hewitt and Theodora living with them, space was at a premium and Agnes had great difficulty managing her new household. (Hugh John, John's son by his first marriage, was by then attending university in Toronto.) But her devotion to her husband made her determined to do her best, and on July 6, 1867, she took out her diary. "I have found something worth living for," she wrote, "living in my Husband's heart and love."

The very next day, however, she began to voice displeasure with John's work habits. "I do wish there could be a law passed forbidding Sunday politics." Yet she was prepared to make the best of the situation:

> I do so like to identify myself with all my husband's pursuits and occupations, he is so busy and so much older than I that I would soon fall out of his life if I went my own ways . . . on the whole I think he likes me near him.

One aspect of his work that she *did* enjoy was the travelling. "I like it very much," she confided to her diary on July 7, 1867. "Everybody pets us up and runs after us delightfully, only sometimes I get tired of being flattered." Even long days spent attending political functions had a certain appeal: she found they made her "long to be alone with him somewhere."

Days spent on her own were less pleasant. The steady flow of mail made her hate the sight of envelopes "addressed in various styles of very pointed feminine hands" and she found answering such "effusions" extremely time consuming.

As a hostess, she did her best to make John proud of her, but she confessed that her efforts on July 9, 1867 had been less than successful. "John says the dinner was a failure. Perhaps my having ordered it to be ready an hour too soon might have had something to do with it."

By November the novelty of being Lady Macdonald had begun to wear off, and Agnes started to face the reality of both her own situation and of John's place in Canadian history. His prominence made her fear that even her diaries would one day become public property, and on November 17 she admitted that she "was afraid of putting anything in these pages which — in time to come — I may find ought not to be written." Even so, she could not refrain from giving future generations a glimpse of the idyllic moments she and John sometimes shared. "Do you think it very wicked of me," she wrote, "to rest my head on his shoulder while he read me 'Locksley Hall'?"

Three weeks later she found that "the excitement of married life is beginning to be more natural," and she described herself as "a laborious housekeeper." Unfortunately, the dissatisfaction and feelings of inadequacy that would haunt the wives of future prime ministers had begun to take a toll on her. Almost overnight she had gone from being what she herself described as an "insignificant young spinster" to a wife deeply in love with her husband and an important figure in Canadian society. The oppressive religious training she had received as a child soon melded with the stringent mores of the Victorian age to cause her moments of consternation. Did she deserve to be so much in love? Was it right to be proud that she was the wife of Canada's first prime minister? She was desperately confused and in January, 1868, wrote: "All my heart's devotion is so entirely given up to [John] that my only fear is such affection is sinful . . ."

At about the same time, John's health became a matter of concern, and to make their life together more relaxing, she asked that he not discuss his work at home. In February, 1868, she also started to discourage his drinking. "I have given up wine," she wrote on February 8, "this is for example's sake and because I think it is unnecessary."

Religion became her mainstay and she told her diary that she was trying to disentangle her life and make her thoughts arrange themselves. On the domestic front, her abilities had improved to the point where she could hold a dinner party that satisfied even John. Outside her home, however, she was less comfortable: large functions made her ill at ease — especially if John did not attend them with her.

But her biggest worry was the discovery that her renunciation of wine had not had the desired effect on John. She felt that she had been "over-confident, vain and presumptious" in feeling that she had the power to curb his drinking. Certainly what was euphemistically referred to as John's "weakness" could not have come as a surprise to her. Her brother, Hewitt, had been aware of John's alcoholism long before the marriage and the newspapers had been publishing stories about it for years.

As the weeks passed, she found even more worries to add to her growing list. She felt that she was not only vain and proud, but that her life was full of idleness. Frivolous pastimes seemed wrong and unsatisfactory to her, and to discipline herself she began to fill her days with Bible study, French lessons and work at the Ottawa Orphan's Home.

Her mind was in constant turmoil. She loved pretty things but considered them sinful. In describing a trip she and John made to Halifax she wrote:

> We were feted everywhere — such constant dissipation as it was, flattering too, but so unsatisfactory and fatiguing, yet I know I liked it all — the prominent part I had to play, the pretty dresses to wear, the compliments to listen to ... All this is bad for the "Truer Life" — I feel how frivolous it makes me.

Yet despite the starchy puritanism that manifested itself from time to time, Agnes possessed a sense of humor. In the winter of 1868, while walking to church, she met a man with a "great frozen spot on his nose" that looked like a piece of dangling cloth. "Fancy our greeting," she wrote in her diary, "after an interchange of bows! — 'Oh excuse me Mr. Desbarats — but — I fear your nose is frozen !!!' "

Moments like this became fewer, however, as her self-doubt grew stronger. Her diary entry for April 19, 1868, shows how deep her introspection had become:

> I know I am very apt to be led astray as to my motives and that analyzing them too much is unhealthy for me, and I also know that my love of power is strong, so strong that sometimes I dread it influences me when I imagine I am influenced by a sense of right.

When D'Arcy McGee, a member of the House of Commons, was assassinated on April 7, 1868, Agnes was horrified.

> The words fell like blows of iron across my heart [she wrote five days later] it was dreadful ... I sat trembling

with fear and horror ... for one could not tell how many more assailants might be lurking in the gray-lit streets.

The thought that John might meet a similar fate was another strain on an already overburdened mind.

Then, in June, her anguish ceased. She was pregnant and her joy knew no bounds. "It seems so wonderful and yet so beautiful," she confided to her diary, "I can hardly express what a new life it has given me." On September 24 she even allowed herself to be smug:

> I often think what an unsatisfactory existence a woman must lead who, passing girlhood and having no particular vocation, never realizes the joys of wife and mother and spends their [sic] lives in trying to fill the void which nature has decreed they should experience.

She began to walk out in the late afternoons to meet John on his way home from work, and when he started using this time together to talk about his political problems, she did not balk. To her surprise she found the conversations stimulating.

Over the years, her interest in politics grew, but she told one man who asked her to intercede on his behalf with John:

> My lord and master who in his private capacity simply lives to please and gratify me to the utmost extent of his power, is *absolutely* tyrannical is his public life so far as I am concerned — If I interfere in any sort of way he will be annoyed, and more, he will be 'disinclined'. I know him *so* well!

Eventually she began voicing her own opinions and wishes on certain issues. "But Sir John, as is usual with him on these domestic occasions, looked very benign[,] very gracious, very pleasant — but — answered not one word! He never does!"

In the meantime, Agnes was basking in the glow of her advancing pregnancy. On January 1, 1869 she wrote:

> I think this was the happiest New Year's Day I can remember since I was a little child and used to have a

holiday and many presents and play and romp in the tropic sunshine of my native land ... About 90 callers. I like so much this old fashioned custom, it is truly kind and cordial and friendly.

Finally, on February 8, after a difficult labor, she gave birth to a girl, Mary. "What words can tell how my heart swells with love and pride as I look at her," Agnes bubbled on April 1. Yet within weeks, a nagging fear had begun to destroy the tranquility of the nursery.

There was something wrong. Mary was not developing normally. Her enlarged head was a sure indication of hydrocephalus, and when the condition was finally diagnosed at the end of the month, Agnes and John were devastated. Mary would live, but she would never walk or be able to take care of herself. Worst of all, her mental development would be slow, and although she was not mentally retarded, her inability to ever speak properly would make her life a trial.

For months Agnes could not unburden herself even to her diary. When she finally did write again in November, her words were terse:

I have suffered keenly in mind ... Only One who knows all our hearts can tell how keenly and painfully or how for long weeks all was gloom and disappointment.

Adding to her problems were John's recurring bouts of drunkenness. Although she realized she could not prevent his drinking, she eventually began spending long evenings in the visitors' gallery of the House of Commons waiting for the sitting to end so she could usher him home before his cronies lured him into the nearest bar.

In the meantime, John's financial affairs had begun to deteriorate. Debts had piled up until his income could no longer cover them, and the situation soon became desperate. This worry, combined with her heavy social commitments, quickly wore Agnes down. To make matters worse, Mary had begun to care more for her nurse than for her parents. On New Year's Day, 1871, Agnes realized how serious the matter had become:

I had charge of my darling Baby all . . . afternoon, and she fretted for her nurse and I felt how wrong this state of things really is, when a child loves so much more dearly a stranger than its own mother, but yet what can be done? I am by no means fashionable . . . yet somehow so many little occupations keep me from my nursery.

Little could be done about either John's drinking or the demands on Agnes' time, but in April, 1872, a group of friends eased John's financial problems by collecting and investing $67,500 in his name. Then, in 1873, Agnes had a second burden lifted when John and his Conservative government resigned.

With her social obligations reduced, Agnes was able to concentrate more fully on the nursery. Both she and John treated Mary as much as possible like a normal child, and as a result she began to develop a pleasing — even cheerful — disposition.

The five years John was out of office passed pleasantly for Agnes. The one dark shadow fell on February 26, 1875, with the death of her mother. "Who can fill her place?" Agnes wrote despairingly. Yet she quickly came to grips with her loss and on March 14 pronounced herself much better.

After that she all but gave up keeping her diary and adapted to the more leisurely pace of her new life. Then, on October 17, 1878, she squared her shoulders as John was once again sworn in as prime minister. Occasionally she listened to the debates in the House of Commons and during one particularly heated session in 1878 over the choice of a new Speaker, stood up in the visitors' gallery, stamped her foot and shouted: "Did ever any person see such tactics!" From that point on she listened to the proceedings with equanimity and when John was ill in 1881 took notes so she could give him a first hand account of the day's activities.

The following year, perhaps as a reward to Agnes for her devoted care, John bought Earnscliffe, a three-storey Gothic Revival mansion they had rented for a year in 1870. Agnes had always loved the house and when it was placed on the market had coaxed John to buy it. They were both delighted with their purchase, and it remained their home until

John's death in 1891.

Although a stable family life had always been what Agnes craved most, she still enjoyed the travelling associated with John's position. When the opportunity arose in 1886 to make a tour of Western Canada, she was delighted. Leaving on July 10, they travelled by private railway car all the way to the Pacific Coast.

The journey was an ideal chance for Agnes to try her hand at writing, and an article, "By Car and by Cowcatcher", was later published by *Murray's Magazine* of London. Its success encouraged Agnes, and she continued to contribute to the magazine for several years.

At once entertaining and informative, her first article tells the story of her impulsive decision to get a better view of Western Canada by travelling on a cowcatcher — the metal frame on the front of a locomotive used to remove obstacles from the tracks.

Her sense of adventure was first sparked in Calgary when she visited the cab of the locomotive. Later, at Laggan Station, she inspected the engine and cowcatcher and decided to make the rest of the journey wrapped in a linen carriage cover viewing nature from a front row seat.

Railway officials were flabbergasted and spectators shocked, but fifty-year-old Agnes braved both landslides and forest fires to see the adventure through to its end. Even though her behaviour was somewhat unorthodox, it was a vast improvement over the early days of her marriage when she had repressed every self-indulgent whim to compensate for her happiness.

But if Agnes's life style was more relaxed, John's was not, and in May, 1891, he suffered a series of strokes. For weeks Agnes assumed many of the nursing responsibilities herself, but the situation was hopeless and on June 6, John died at the age of seventy-six.

To temporarily fill the void, Agnes concentrated on trying to have Sir Charles Tupper named to succeed her husband as prime minister. On the night of John's death, she wrote to the Governor General, Lord Stanley, urging him to ask Sir Charles to form a new government.

Stanley, however, had his own ideas and immediately called upon Sir John Thompson, Justice Minister in the

Macdonald Cabinet. The move infuriated Agnes who had never been able to get along with Thompson. (In letters to his wife, Thompson had called Agnes a "mole catcher" and declared her "ugly as sin".)

To her credit, Agnes had a better reason than personal dislike for objecting to Stanley's choice of Thompson. She feared that Ontario Protestants would desert the Conservative Party if Thompson, a Methodist turned Catholic, took over as leader. "It is not so much his religion," she later wrote to Sir Charles Tupper, "as the fact of being a pervert." (She meant, of course, convert.)

In the end, Thompson declined the offer and Senator John Abbott stepped forward as the new prime minister. For Agnes it was the lesser of two evils. She felt that Abbott was too old for the job and correctly guessed that his leadership would be weak and indecisive.

Later that year, Agnes took stock of her financial affairs (John had overcome his difficulties and left her well provided for) and left Earnscliffe to begin a life of aimless wandering.

Her only consolation during the long years that followed was the title Queen Victoria bestowed upon her in recognition of John's distinguished public service. As Baroness Macdonald of Earnscliffe, Agnes was entitled to certain privileges and after leaving with Mary for England she took up a new social life that saw her mingling with members of the Royal Family and attending debates in the House of Lords. Although England would remain her official country of residence until her death, she went each year for visits to the Continent.

Nothing, however, provided a cure for her restlessness, and in 1893 she admitted "the joy has somehow gone out of my life." A year later she was still grieving:

> Nothing happens to me [she wrote to John's brother-in-law, James Williamson] even the most trifling event in my every day life occurs, but it brings a sickening longing to have him near to tell it to, as I used in the happy days gone by!

Despite her travels, she continued to follow the Canadian political scene, and when Mackenzie Bowell was sworn in as prime minister following the death of Sir John Thompson (who had succeeded Abbott) in 1894, she let her feelings be known. "I never liked him," she said, "and he never liked me. We were greatly antagonistic by nature."

When the demand of office finally proved too much for Bowell, Agnes was delighted to learn that Sir Charles Tupper, the man she had wanted to succeed John in 1891, had taken over as prime minister. Although she had privately criticized Tupper's "peculiar methods," she felt that his "true and lofty sense of duty" was exactly what Canada needed.

Meanwhile, in England, the suffragette movement had attracted Agnes's attention, but despite her own interest in politics, she was thoroughly repelled by what she saw. "They are disgusting everybody," she said, "but indeed their existence and proceedings are the outcome of the extraordinary prominence encouraged in women of all classes in England of late years." Her opinion of Canadian suffragettes was equally low, and she could muster no sympathy for their cause.

On the domestic front, Mary had improved, and Agnes began to find her "companionable — very gentle but with very fixed ways and wishes." In 1899 she wrote to a friend saying that in the event of her death she wanted Mary to "be taken back to Canada . . . her home [is] not to be in Ottawa." Eleven years later she changed her mind and decided that because Mary had grown to love England, she should be allowed to stay there in her own home and with her own staff.

For Agnes the lonely ramblings continued until 1920 when she suffered a series of strokes. Although she survived the initial crisis, her condition deteriorated, and she died at Eastbourne, near London, on September 5 at the age of eighty-four.

JANE MACKENZIE

In 1850 Jane Sym's world was bound by the perimeter of her father's Ontario farm. The endless routine of keeping house and looking after her younger brothers and sisters left little time for a life of her own, and despite her graceful build and delicate features, she seemed destined for the fate that most 19th century women feared above all — spinsterhood.

Then, at the age of twenty-five, she met Alexander Mackenzie, a stonemason and contractor who walked eight miles every Sunday to attend a small Baptist church near the Sym's farm in the township of Sarnia. One day after service, Jane's father invited Mackenzie home for lunch, and although the young Scotsman spent most of his time talking about politics and his invalid wife, he at least took note of Jane's existence.

As time passed, the health of Mackenzie's wife, Helen, deteriorated and on January 4, 1852, she died at the age of twenty-five. Mackenzie, left with a three-year-old daughter, began to look more closely at Jane whose quiet way of going about her work sparked first his admiration and later his affection, and they were married on June 17, 1853.

Unfortunately, few firsthand accounts of Jane's life exist and it is virtually impossible to gain insight into her thoughts and feelings. No diary has been passed into the public record and most of the intimate glimpses we get come from letters written by Alexander.

That he was in love with Jane is certain. In a letter to his "dearest Jeannie" dated March 2, 1880, he told her that at the time of their marriage:

Jane Mackenzie

. . . I liked you for what I believed you was [sic]. Now I love you for what I know you are . . . I had no doubt you would make my life happy or at least would do your best to do so. Now I can say you have more than realized my hopes and expectations and I look back on 27 years of happiest married life and I look forward with cheerfulness to what remains to us of life on this earth . . . My warmest love you had before, but that commanded my admiration and I daily receive the strongest evidence that no one ever had a stronger hold on all hearts than you have here. I am very proud of all this. I always feel backward in language of a demonstrative character and will only say what I always think that I have the best of wives, God bless her.

Written two years after his term as prime minister had expired, the letter shows that their relationship was warm and caring. Certainly Jane had not expected when she first married Mackenzie that she would become what the Toronto *Globe* later described as "one of the best-known women of Canada . . . and one of the most admired and respected." Born on March 22, 1825, in Bathurst township, Lanark County, Ontario, she was the daughter of Robert Sym and his wife, Agnes Wylie.

Sym, a native of Scotland, settled in Perth, Ontario, in 1821 and in 1837 moved farther west to Lambton on the southern end of Lake Huron. It was during the years in Perth that Agnes died, leaving Jane to take over as head of the household. No doubt the heavy responsibilities she assumed before the age of twelve robbed Jane of many of the pleasures of childhood, and it has been suggested by biographers of Mackenzie that by the time she was twenty-five, Jane showed in both her manner and appearance heavy traces of her self-sacrificing existence.

Unfortunately, marriage — at least during the early years — made few significant changes in her way of life. She immediately assumed charge of Mackenzie's five-year-old daughter, Mary, and began running a new household in Sarnia. About the only thing she had to adapt to was her husband's contradictory nature.

Thin-lipped and gaunt, Mackenzie had refused when marrying his first wife to repeat the vow "with this body I thee worship." As long as he lived he made family prayers a vital part of his daily routine, and many people considered him too strait-laced for his own good. Yet despite his austerity, he had in his earlier years played practical jokes with abandon and during his courtship of Helen had shown his reckless courage by picking his way across rotten ice floes just for the pleasure of seeing her.

By 1851 he had begun to take an interest in politics, and for the first years of their marriage saw little of Jane as he campaigned for George Brown, a man whose views matched his own. With no other outlet for her energy, Jane let her world revolve around her home and devoted herself to taking care of Mary.

Then, in 1861, Mackenzie ran successfully as a Liberal candidate for the Legislative Assembly of Canada. Although little is known of Jane's personal life, it is clear from newspaper accounts of the time that she did not take an active part in her husband's campaigning. Reserved by nature, she preferred to remain at home on familiar territory. Mary on the other hand enjoyed appearing with her father and by 1870 was attending rallies and picnics as he campaigned successfully first for a seat in the House of Commons and then in the Legislative Assembly of Ontario.

One of Jane's few public appearances during this period came on election day 1871 when a victory parade marched up to her front doorstep. Alone, she went out to tell the crowd that because the general swing toward the Liberals had made her husband confident of victory, he had already left for Ottawa to assume his new duties.

Although Jane's feelings toward Alexander's career were never made public, one incident makes it clear that she did not share Agnes Macdonald's enthusiasm for politics. As she sat chatting late in December, 1871 with a Presbyterian minister, a letter arrived for her from Ottawa. She read it in silence as a tear trickled down her cheek. Then, unable to speak, she handed the letter to her guest. It was from Alexander, announcing his appointment to the Cabinet as Treasurer of Ontario and asking her to pray for him that he might "be kept right amid the temptations and difficulties of this responsible position."

It *was* a responsible position. But if Jane — who was childless — had accepted her husband's long campaign trips, she was not about to accept the endless weeks he would now have to spend in Ottawa — at least not quietly. "I have been only five days at home for six months," Mackenzie told a friend in May, 1872, "and my wife utters an occasional protest." Unfortunately, Jane's feelings in this regard seem to have meant very little and during the next six months she saw even less of him. To make matters worse, Mary was married later that year, leaving Jane totally alone.

Then, in November, 1873, Mackenzie who in March had become leader of the federal Opposition was called upon to form the first Liberal administration of the Dominion after the downfall of Macdonald and his Conservatives. He quickly found a house on Kent Street in Ottawa, not far from the West Block, and arranged for Jane to join him.

For Jane, then forty-eight, the transformation from housewife to society leader must have been painful. Yet with careful coaching, she adapted well to her new role and received guests graciously. According to the *Globe*, she stepped quietly "from a sphere of comparative humbleness to the exalted position of wife of the first minister of the Dominion" and acquitted "herself of the duties that fell to her in a manner that won for her praise and admiration from all quarters."

Despite their Baptist life style, she and Alexander surprised their guests by serving champagne and other wines at their many dinner parties, and Jane even learned to dance. Friends from Sarnia were always welcome, and Conservatives were received just as warmly as Liberals.

According to William Buckingham, Mackenzie's secretary, Jane was the perfect political hostess:

> While at Ottawa Mrs. Mackenzie had to play a chief role in a brilliant circle. It was what may be called the *renaissance* period of our social life, and the Court she graced was in point of munificence and splendour unexampled in the history of the Dominion. In that supreme moment she showed how well she merited her husband's confidence and love — how nobly she was qualified to help and support him in every phase of his varying life. She was not dazzled by the light, but took

29

her place, as he had taken his, with a quiet dignity and kindliness, frankness and charm of manner which disarmed criticism and conquered every heart.

Regardless of how Jane felt personally about her new role, Buckingham's grandiloquent account indicates that she at least put on a good front. Then, in 1874, her staying power was tested to the limit. A fire broke out in their home and within minutes their clothing, furniture and personal papers had been totally destroyed.

In the days that followed, they rented a new house, Cliffside, and tried to put the horror of the fire behind them. It was much easier for Alexander who had the demands of government to fill his days than it was for Jane, and in August she left on a badly needed trip to the seashore.

Although the letters Alexander wrote during this brief separation have been preserved, Jane's have not, and we get at best a one-sided view of their relationship during this period. At times the unilateral nature of the existing correspondence is extremely frustrating: it is like playing chess with an opponent who uses invisible pieces.

Certainly the man who wrote asking his wife to pardon him for writing again after having written the day before and who facetiously promised not to sin again for some time, was far removed from the dour Scotsman who stared down his opponents every day in the House of Commons.

On August 9, after returning home from church, Mackenzie brought up "all arrears in domestic correspondence" and saved the last and best for his "beloved wife":

> The question [he wrote] is where are you? I presume you are vindicating your title to the Baptist profession by immersing well and thus at once sticking to your principles and laying in a store of health for the winter. A horrible thought just strikes me, however, what if you should now suddenly grow fat and become the 'Gross Feme' [sic] of the family!! [As time had passed, Jane's figure had filled out and her features had assumed a softness not evident in her early years.] To be sure we could sing in our misery As she grew fat he grew lean.

Ha Ha. . . No doubt the compensatory laws of nature are very admirable and it may be satisfactory to know that we keep the weight between us, but I would rather carry my own share of it.

Later in the letter, Mackenzie became more thoughtful:

There is nothing I long for so much as to get one month in the hills of Scotland with you, to show you each familiar knoll and loch which I often passed in life's young dream; there seems little chance of realizing that longing but we will live in hope . . . I am ambitious, or anxious rather, to have it in my power to spend a little time with you when and where the anxieties of public life will not have an existence. . . I suppose I need hardly write you at all as these letters may not reach you, but when you are away and I at home I always feel uneasy and like to write.

To keep this sentiment from getting out of hand, he tried to tone the last paragraph of the letter down:

. . . you may come to the conclusion that I cannot get on alone. You don't flatter yourself with such a notion. You see there is such a luxury in doing what I please just as I please . . . good night my dear Jane.

From you ever affectionate husband

A. Mackenzie

The next day a letter from Jane sent his spirits soaring and he immediately picked up his pen.

My beloved wife

I received your letter today from Quebec. I wrote you on Saturday and again last night. If your letter had not come I thought of advertising for you as 'a disconsolate husband would be glad to hear tidings of his wife who left Ottawa the morning of the 4th and has not since been heard of. Her age about — , skin fair,

31

hair mixed, teeth good and nearly new. Small, fat, docile disposition and had $30 in her pocket. Do you think this would find you(?). . .

Mr. Buckingham and I use up a handkerchief daily. I think of using a towel after this for economical reasons. If you stay away long it may come to a shirt. I have made up my mind to deprive you of your servant man this week. I found this morning that the nice gentleman was using the spare bedroom since you left. His impudence is unbounded . . .

Mr. Macdonald is well and so is your liege lord (if it be not presumptuous for any man nowadays to call himself a woman's lord.)

Your ever affectionate husband

A. Mackenzie

Although the letters do not give the insight into Jane's personality that those she wrote to Alexander undoubtedly did, they do indicate that despite her reserve she enjoyed being teased (either that or Mackenzie was a sado-masochist!) and had a sense of humor.

In the spring of 1875 they decided to take the long awaited trip to England and Scotland. Mixing business with pleasure, they paid a formal call on Queen Victoria in London, then left for Paris. They arrived in Scotland in July and for ten days rested in Pitlochry, Alexander's birthplace.

Although invitations to visit other parts of the country arrived daily, they accepted only two: Mackenzie wanted to return to Greenock, the port he had sailed from when he immigrated to Canada in 1842, and Irvine, where he had met his first wife. What Jane's thoughts were in visiting the home of her predecessor remain unknown, but it is not improbable that she felt an acute pang of jealousy in discovering that after twenty-three years her husband retained so strong an attachment to his first wife that he could still sentimentalize over the place of their first meeting.

After their return to Canada, Mackenzie faced a round of engagements that took him frequently away from Ottawa. Jane, who did not share Agnes Macdonald's fondness for political junkets, stayed home and kept up-to-date on·her husband's activities by letter.

Occasionally articles appeared in the newspapers while he was away that upset Mackenzie and, fearful lest Jane should believe the derogatory comments made about him, he tried to justify himself to her:

> Do not believe the Tory papers [he implored her] when they describe me as eaten up with ambition. I think I know myself and I can honestly say that my only ambition is to succeed in governing the country well and without reproach.

Jane's opinion was obviously important to him, but it seems strange that after so many years of marriage Mackenzie felt that her faith in him could be shaken by petty attacks in opposition newspapers. Whether it was her faith he questioned or his own is difficult to determine, but by 1877 he had enough self-confidence to launch a vigorous program of precampaign electioneering.

In August, accompanied by Mary and Jane, he set off on a gruelling tour of the Maritimes. Jane's presence can be explained in one of three ways: she may have overcome her reserve and dislike of campaigning or she may have been concerned enough for Mackenzie's health, which had been failing for some time, to want to keep an eye on him. It is also conceivable that the attention she had attracted as a parliamentary hostess had increased her political value and thus made her very presence on the platform a boost for the Liberal cause.

The latter two possibilities seem the most likely, especially in view of the fact that as her husband's strength ebbed in 1878 she stepped up the pace of her activities and held a series of drawing rooms.

The one break in the long campaign came on June 17 when she and Alexander invited a few close friends to celebrate their silver wedding anniversary with them. Things did not go as planned, however, and as the evening progressed people who had heard of the celebration but had not been invited began arriving with gifts.

Mackenzie, who felt the presents compromised his

position as prime minister, asked one of the offenders to take the parcel away. "My evening's enjoyment with a few friends is utterly destroyed," he complained, "by the sending of presents. I must beg of you to take your own back . . . This is the greatest favour you can do me. I never felt so mortified in my life. It looks as if we had got the little evening party up on purpose. Pray let nothing deter you from yielding to my wishes."

Everyone tried to laugh the matter off, but the evening was ruined, and the next morning Jane was told to have all the gifts wrapped up and returned.

In the end, not even Mackenzie's high-minded scruples could win him reelection. The Liberal Party was soundly defeated and on September 17 he stepped aside as Sir John A. Macdonald again took over as prime minister.

Given Jane's fondness for a quiet domestic life, it is likely that she was privately pleased with the results of the election. Three days after the votes were tallied, however, she received a letter from the Governor General, Lord Dufferin, in which he commiserated with her over the loss:

> Of course [he wrote] you must have been disappointed at the result of the elections, but no feeling of mortification need mingle with the surprise the result has occasioned.

Disappointed or not, the Mackenzies moved to Toronto where house hunting proved to be almost as arduous as campaigning had been. Without the income they had received when Alexander was prime minister, they could not afford an elaborate house and whenever they approached the owner of a place they considered suitable, they found the price suddenly skyrocketed. Mackenzie's face was recognized everywhere and it appeared that potential sellers were determined to profit from his political misfortunes.

Finally he planned a counterattack. Jane was not as widely known and together they began strolling past prospective houses scanning them closely from rooftop to doorstep. Whenever they saw one they liked, Mackenzie continued around the block while Jane went back, knocked on the door and asked for the grand tour. Nothing really pleased them, however, and on the day they signed a bill of sale it was more out of desperation than because they had found the place of their dreams.

In the meantime, Mackenzie had decided to stay on as leader of the Opposition and in January, 1879, celebrated his fifty-seventh birthday. A letter he wrote thanking a friend for a pair of suspenders gives a charming glimpse of the more lighthearted moments he and Jane shared together:

> The postman has just left your package, enclosing your kind note and your contribution towards 'bracing' me up for my coming duties.
>
> My wife looked anxiously over my shoulder at the mysterious package as I opened it, observing, no doubt, the lady's handwriting, and fearing probably that it was a love-philtre which might chain me to the fair correspondent. . .
>
> At the first glance she said 'garters! What can it mean?' I replied in the words of the motto of the Order of the Garter, as well as of the Sovereigns of England: 'Evil be to him that evil thinks' 'Honi soit qui mal y pense,' But when the whole was unfolded, and your note dropped out, I think all her fears vanished, and I was graciously permitted to acknowledge the present myself . . .

Although life in Toronto freed Jane of many of the pressures of the Ottawa social scene, it meant that she and Alexander were frequently separated. His letters kept her abreast of the proceedings in the House of Commons, but whether she was really interested is another matter.

By the spring of 1880 she was anxious to go to Ottawa and spend some time with him. An outbreak of smallpox, however, delayed her visit, and in a letter written on March 2, Mackenzie told her how much he missed her. A few paragraphs later he made an interesting though passing reference to the help she had been to him throughout his career. "In trying circumstances," he wrote, "you nobly did your share in maintaining my position."

Eight weeks later he retired as leader of the Opposition and began to plan a trip to Europe. Sailing in May, 1881, he hoped for a smooth crossing, but it was not to be. Jane was ill during the entire voyage and only managed to rally when the English coast appeared on the horizon.

In Switzerland, she was so overwhelmed by the beauty of the Alps that she insisted over her husband's objections that they travel to Lucerne to see the sun rise on the Rigi. The steep incline of the railway track took them quickly up the mountain and before long a spectacular view spread out beneath them. Unfortunately it was a little too spectacular in places, and when Jane began to sense that any untoward movement could send them plummeting to their deaths, her enthusiasm waned. That night she was unable to sleep and when she woke up the next morning it was to find that storm clouds, which had deposited seven inches of snow during the night, would obscure the sunrise and make the entire expedition an exercise in futility.

It did not lessen their desire to see all they could of Europe, and in 1883 they made a third trip, focussing on the country Jane most wanted to see — Italy. As it turned out, it was their last trip to the Continent. After their return to Toronto they were told by a doctor that Mackenzie's nervous system had been irreparably impaired by the long years in politics, and they decided to buy a new house on Wellesley Street in a quieter district of Toronto between Yonge Street and the Legislative Buildings. Every day they went out walking together, but it was Jane, by far the stronger of the two, who offered her arm to Alexander.

As the years passed, Jane led an unobtrusive life nursing her husband as his health continued to deteriorate. According to Buckingham, those closest to her commented on the "fortitude and cheerfulness" with which she "assisted and sustained" Mackenzie during his last years.

After his death on April 17, 1892, she declined a state pension and later requested that the proceeds of a testimonial fund that had been collected by political friends be applied toward the endowment of the Mackenzie scholarship in political science awarded by Toronto and McGill Universities.

She continued to live quietly in her home on Wellesley Street, far away from the public eye. Then, early in the spring of 1893, her health began to fail. The condition was diagnosed as inflammation of the bowel, and after a brief illness, she died on March 30 at the age of sixty-eight.

MARY ABBOTT

Mary Bethune, who married John Joseph Caldwell Abbott in 1849, has the distinction of being the most obscure wife of a prime minister in Canadian history. Not even the date of her birth has been determined with any accuracy, and her father, James G. Bethune, has been variously described as a lawyer and the Anglican Dean of Montreal.

About all that is known with any certainty — other than the date of her marriage — is that she was the mother of eight children. According to sources at the Prime Ministers' Archives, Manuscript Division, Public Archives of Canada, no further details, either published or unpublished, have ever been discovered concerning her life. Not even the date of her death can be determined from their records.

If, as Homer counselled, the Abbotts were a husband and wife who kept their "household in oneness of mind," Mary's preference for a quiet life is perhaps mirrored in a comment made by her husband after being chosen to succeed Sir John A. Macdonald as prime minister in 1891:

> I hate politics and what are considered their appropriate measures. I hate notoriety, public meetings, public speeches, caucuses, and everything that I know of which is apparently the necessary incident of politics — except doing public work to the best of my ability. Why should I go where the doing of public work will only make me hated . . . and where I can gain reputation and credit by practising arts which I detest to acquire popularity?

Purported to be Mary Abbott

With such an inimical attitude to the burden that had been thrust upon him by those who considered him "not particularly obnoxious to anybody," it is not surprising that Abbott served a mere seventeen months before retiring to private life.

ANNIE THOMPSON

Lady Thompson, wife of Canada's fourth prime minister, differed little from her alter ego, Annie Affleck, the Halifax shop assistant. Certainly she was older, stouter and much more cynical, but her two most distinguishing characteristics — her homeyness and her overwhelming need to love and be loved — remained unchanged.

Born in Halifax on June 26, 1845, Anna E. Affleck was the daughter of Captain James Affleck and his wife, Catherine Saunders. Affleck, a seaman from Berwick-upon-Tweed, England, immigrated to Canada in 1840 and settled in Halifax where he met his future wife, a native of Newfoundland.

Although little is known about James other than the fact that he was lost at sea on a voyage to the West Indies in 1870, J. Castell Hopkins, biographer of Sir John Thompson, has suggested that the father-in-law of the future prime minister was not wealthy. Thompson "won and wedded his wife," Hopkins wrote in 1895, "... and being the man he was, it is probable that he never even considered the fact that her lack of money made the future depend entirely upon his own exertions."

Male chauvinism notwithstanding, Annie and John probably met for the first time in 1866. Although Annie had other suitors, she took an especial interest in Thompson, who had recently been admitted to the bar of Nova Scotia, and within a year their courtship had begun in earnest.

In a diary she kept for six months in 1867, Annie gives a glimpse not only of the early stages of their courtship, but also

Annie Thompson

of her own high-strung, rather hypochondrical nature. Sometimes she and Thompson went for long walks together; occasionally they spent evenings with friends in her parents' drawing room. But for a young woman in love, Annie was not always in the best of spirits. "I seem to live one day after another," she wrote on July 6, "neither useful in this world nor preparing for the next." It had taken thirty-one-year-old Agnes Macdonald almost twelve months of marriage to lapse into such moods of self-deprecation.

As the summer progressed, Annie saw more and more of Thompson and they began to study French and shorthand together. Yet her moods were unpredictable. She devoted a great deal of time to worrying — unnecessarily it seems — about her health. In late July not even walks with Thompson in the "glorious moonlight" could keep her from fretting about what she referred to as "weak" spells.

On July 24 she confided to her diary that she had passed the day "without doing much of anything but thinking a great deal and that is not very pleasant." Gradually she began to complain of being "cross and disagreeable" even when Thompson was with her, and the impression she conveys throughout the entire diary is that no matter how much attention he paid her, it was not enough. "Thompson in we had a talk," she wrote on November 14," and I would almost of [sic] fought with him if he could of [sic] taken any notice of me." But even though such peevishness would have discouraged most men, it did not deter Thompson: Annie *did* have her good days and on December 14 she reported, "I feel more contented than I have for some time."

During the early months of 1868 she spent most of her time sewing and working on her French and shorthand. Although little else is known about Annie's activities during this period, Lady Aberdeen, wife of Canada's seventh governor general, recorded in her journal on December 13, 1894 that ". . . Lady Thompson was employed for a time in some capacity in a shop at Halifax." It is possible that after Captain Affleck's death in 1870, Annie found it necessary to help her mother, who had been left with several young children, by taking the then unfashionable step of going to work.

Whatever the case, she went on seeing Thompson and their relationship continued along much the same path it had in 1867. In a letter to Annie dated May 30, 1886, Thompson recalled

> the evening about 18 years ago when you wore curls (Sunday) and were so mad with me that you could hardly keep from crying — because you thought that I did not take very much notice of you on the way home from church although I had gone two miles just to look at you.

Despite Annie's sulking, Thompson adored her, and on July 5, 1870 the two were married in Portland, Maine. Arranging the ceremony had not been easy. John was a Methodist, Annie a Catholic, and so-called mixed marriages were not then permitted in Halifax. As a result, the two were advised by a canon of the Roman Catholic Church to go to Portland where the local bishop would perform the ceremony. Mrs. Affleck and Annie left Halifax early in July and on the 5th Annie and John were married in the bishop's parlor.

The following year John took two more important steps: he joined the Catholic Church and ran successfully for Halifax City Council. On the domestic front, he and Annie settled down to a happy life together and developed so intimate a relationship that even the briefest separations were all but unbearable.

Their first child, John, was born on October 20, 1872, and when a business matter took Thompson to Saint John, New Brunswick, the following May, he was miserable at being so far from his family. On the 22nd he wrote to Annie telling her how homesick he was and how he yearned "to hear little buttons squall and above all . . . to have a lot of hugs from my own poor little dolly that I am so very, very fond of."

A second son, Joseph, was born in 1874 and a daughter, Mary Aloysia (Babe), in 1876. While conducting business in Amherst, Nova Scotia, in September, 1874, John sat down to answer several letters he had received from Annie.

> I was glad . . . that you cried about me but you poor pet when I came to the part where you said the house

looked so big and the children so little I had to laugh right out. Now you must not be cross with me. I know I have not made you as happy and comfortable as I might but never mind pet you know I love you ever so much more than I can tell you . . .

In 1877 John, by then a well-respected lawyer, was elected as a Conservative to the Legislative Assembly of Nova Scotia. Although his financial situation should have been secure, the burden of supporting not only his mother, but also his mother-in-law and several of her children kept him heavily in debt.

His appointment to the provincial cabinet in 1878 did little to improve the situation; in fact, it created its own set of problems by taking him frequently away from Halifax. The strain took its toll on Annie, and after the birth of their second daughter, Mary Helena (Lena), on March 29, 1878, she was often ill. Yet she delighted in her family, and in a letter to John dated September 6, 1878, she told him how the children "all wanted to get in bed with me last night and they were awake long before daybreak throwing boots at one another and sitting on my head . . ."

The next two years were especially trying for Annie: a third daughter, born on November 19, 1879, died on August 17, 1880, while a son died a few hours after his birth on December 9, 1880. Not surprisingly, her spirits were low.

I wonder you had patience with me the other morning you poor pet, [she wrote to John on June 21, 1881] you have troubles enough without my bothering you too; now you must not think about me at all[.] I am feeling better today and when I get over this nervous fit I will be all right.

On October 23, while John was attending a session of the Supreme Court in Ottawa, she wrote: ". . . if you only knew how much we are all like orphans when you are away . . ." A few days later her spirits improved and she told him about a social call she had made with John, Jr.: ". . . while we were waiting for the servant to go upstairs John wanted to know if the silver was better than ours . . ."

On the 29th their financial situation and John's political future were foremost on her mind.

> I don't see why we can't find a gold mine when we want it so much . . . I would dearly like to see you . . . with a big house, plenty of servants and the best table that money can set for you . . . and then settle down afterwards but as we won't find the mine you would only feel miserable wanting to do lots of things and not being able to afford them.

Her sudden mood swings seem to have been contagious, and a few days later she received a melancholy letter from John. Trying to console him as he so often had consoled her, she told him not to "get dull" and exhorted him to be "just as stiff as they are stout who cares for those grand judges or for anyone else in Ottawa for that matter." A month and a half later, on December 17, she gave birth to another daughter, Frances, who, crippled by a childhood illness, soon became the family pet.

On the political front, John's fortunes were on the rise and the following May he was chosen to succeed Simon Holmes as premier of Nova Scotia. But if John's star was on the rise, that of the Conservative Party was not and during the election campaign that followed, John recognized that his tenure might be very short.

> You want to know how I will feel if you are beaten. [Annie wrote to him on June 14] Well child except for you being disappointed and bored to death not one row of pins . . . I wouldn't mind much if you put in your hat . . . tomorrow.

As it turned out, the Conservatives *were* defeated, and John was appointed to the Supreme Court of Nova Scotia where he served for three years before being named Minister of Justice in the Cabinet of Sir John A. Macdonald. Foremost among his reasons for accepting the portfolio was Annie. Although she had said in 1882 that she didn't care if he gave up politics, her feelings in 1885 were far different. Not only had she come to recognize John's potential, she wanted him to go as far as he could: for one thing, it would improve the family's financial situation.

> . . . I've spent all the evening since tea over [my bills] and they seem to grow [she wrote to him]. It is quite enough to discourage a person. I find that even if we could live on the wind for 3 months that it would take all my allowance to get out of debt. However I must do the best that I can and perhaps we'll manage better this year.

Once John had taken up his duties in Ottawa, Annie, who stayed with the children in Halifax, came face to face with the incubus she feared more than insolvency: loneliness. To make him seem closer to her, she followed his political activities with great interest and expected a letter from him every day. When he did not write she was beside herself. "I wanted to kill someone," she wrote late in 1885, ". . . I must have a letter every day that is all I stipulate."

John valued her letters just as much as she did his and he missed her terribly. "I could not stand the depression so long as this," he told her on September 25, 1885, "but for the feeling all the time that you wished me to do what I have done."

Two months later he found himself in even worse straits when a bout of kidney stones laid him low for several days. Annie, concerned that he was not receiving proper care, immediately made plans to join him in Ottawa. Just before she boarded the train, however, a telegram arrived from John urging her to stay in Halifax. Hurt and angry, she waited until she knew he had recovered, then indulged in a week of constant sulking. John immediately tried to placate her.

> I fear that you are annoyed at my telegraphing for you not to come [he wrote on November 15] . . . My complaint was one that a woman is supposed to know nothing about and I did not want [you] to make your first appearance at Ottawa under these circumstances.

Annie was not convinced and, still smarting from what she saw as John's rebuff, refused to let the matter drop. Once again he tried to make peace.

46

The doctor . . . told me I should only be laid up one day. . . Now as for the awkwardness I spoke of I meant it would be very awkward for you to come to my boarding house which is not good enough for you. When you come I want you to make a better start. As to the looking strange I meant that by the time you would reach Ottawa — Thursday evening — I would be able to be out as the doctor assured me. People would have supposed I had brought you up on a false alarm then they would know you came in consequence of my illness . . .

But Annie was still as insecure as she had been in 1867, and she believed that he had stopped her from joining him because he no longer loved her. It appears that she even accused him of having been interested at some time in another woman. John was beside himself.

Oh my darling [he expostulated on the 22nd] you need not ask me to tell you how I love you! I laid awake most of last night regretting all the time I have been ugly and cross to you . . . But, love, for the things that you used to blame me for I was not to blame. There never for a moment was anyone, the thought of whom ever came between my love and you. If I kept things to myself it was not because there was anything that could make jealousy but because what sometimes seemed to me to be a matter of necessity seemed to annoy you and to give rise to misunderstanding.

Finally Annie was satisfied and domestic harmony was restored. John, however, continued to be miserably homesick and on November 27 tried to explain his situation to his 11-year-old son, Joe: "I feel a good deal like you will when you go away to school . . . That is Mama's fault however — that I am here."

His depression continued and on January 21, 1886, Annie wrote a stern letter.

Oh my Pet my Pet

Cant [sic] you bully things out when I am trying to do

so . . . Baby you break my heart, if you dont [sic] try to be more of a boss, and look this thing in the face and make the best of it for a little while until I can be with you; I think even at the long distance that we are from each other, a sympathy still makes us alike. On Sunday too, as it rained and stormed I thought if only I could be with you long enough just to kiss and hug you and run my hands through your hair, that I would be satisfied . . . You know dear that for myself I have no ambition for any thing in this world but your love, having that I have everything that I want but you know I am so proud of you that, even if I am doing wrong, I cannot help pushing you on, and please God it will turn out all right . . .

The constant flurry of letter writing intrigued Annie's twenty-two-year-old sister, Frances, who wrote to John describing Annie's lucubrations.

Annie has just turned into an immense sheet of paper, bottle of ink and bad pen since you left — at the slightest provocation she takes up arms, and I suppose pours her woes, real or imaginary into your sympathetic ears. She is at it now and will be until the wee sma' hours . . .

If Annie enjoyed writing letters, she enjoyed reading those she received from John even more, and one Sunday evening late in January, 1886, when the children were asleep, she took out a bundle of them, sat down by the fire and read them through. The memories they evoked made her unusually reflective and she immediately wrote a note to John.

I think I must have grown very worldly and hardened my heart very much when I sent you away as I did. Perhaps in old times I was not worldly enough and cared too little for anything outside of you and the children and the house . . . by and bye when we get old we'll settle down into our old way of living for one another first.

A few days later Annie decided to go to Ottawa to

attend the new session of Parliament. Only too aware of how the strain might affect her, John sent a letter of instruction on January 29.

> . . . you *must* come at least a week before the opening. There will be no danger then of you having to go alone — but if you should go alone you are game for it. You are to make sure too to get yourself nice dresses for the opening, for evenings and for the hotel. You may use them or not as you like but you know there is nothing so embarrassing as to feel that one is shabby and . . . not [feeling] embarrassed is making a start. There will be enough to embarrass even with all in one's favor that he can obtain. Now pet remember these are commands not mere advice.

The visit went off well and after enjoying their time together, they were both dejected when Annie returned to Halifax. "I had a wretched day yesterday," John wrote to her on May 31, "feeling as if I could get no rest unless I could get my head on your shoulder." On July 6 he felt like giving her "a good kiss and a slap for writing such short letters."

Annie missed him just as much, but despite her loneliness she could not be induced to make more frequent trips to Ottawa. "Everybody here seemed to expect you would be up with me this time," John told her on August 23. "You should but I tell them next month you are coming."

As time passed he continued to make excuses, while Annie — either because she disliked being away from home or because she felt out of place in Ottawa — managed to come up with abundant reasons for staying in Halifax.

In the meantime, John had adjusted to his new role as Minister of Justice and was making a name for himself in the highest circles. Knighted in 1888, he turned down the governor general's invitation to form a new government following the death of Sir John A. Macdonald in June, 1891 on the grounds that his conversion to Catholicism might lead to difficulties for the Conservative Party. Abbott stepped in briefly to fill the void, but with his resignation in 1892 it became clear that Thompson was the only man for the job.

For Annie it meant being dragged off the sidelines of John's political life and pushed onto the playing field. As the wife of the prime minister, she was expected to take an active part in the capital's social activities — personal aversion notwithstanding.

Certainly her position was far from enviable. According to Lady Aberdeen, people snubbed Annie during her early months in Ottawa because they heard she had once worked as a shop assistant. To make matters worse, John was expected to use his $9,000 a year salary to cover all his official entertainment expenses.

As preposterous as the situation was, Annie vowed to make the best of it. In 1894 she confided to Lady Aberdeen, one of her few friends in Ottawa, how she had helped ease the financial burden.

> Lady T. was telling me tonight [Lady Aberdeen wrote in her diary on December 13, 1894] of some of her plans for managing to eke out their income . . . The winter before last . . . she actually cooked all the dinners for all the members who dined with her husband, some 250 in number, instead of getting a good cook — & they are supposed always to have done things nicely.

Lady Aberdeen then went on to draw a thumbnail sketch of Annie.

> She is a woman by herself at Ottawa & has naturally not made many friends there, being so taken up with her husband & children & not being of the kidney of the society people there . . . But people are very much mistaken who think her merely a domestic woman, knowing nothing of politics or the world outside. She is unfortunately a bit cynical & looks upon politics as a game of chess, but she has a clear head & good judgement & has been of infinite use to Sir John . . . for he was perhaps too much disposed to believe everyone as good as himself.

In April, 1894, while organizing the first annual meeting of the newly formed National Council of Women of Canada, Lady Aberdeen persuaded Annie and Zoë Laurier, wife of the future prime minister, Wilfrid Laurier, to serve as joint vice-presidents. John recognized both the benefit the appointment would be to Annie socially and the good the council would do for the women of Canada, and he agreed to address the opening meeting.

The council, he said, would "conduce to the best welfare of the country, by promoting greater unity of thought, sympathy and purpose, amongst women workers of all classes and sections of the people."

Not long after, his health began to deteriorate and he was advised by three doctors to give up all political activity for a year. Annie urged him to resign, but he refused, saying that any such action on his part would be cowardly. Instead, he agreed to reduce his workload and to go to Europe on a combined business and pleasure trip.

As much as he wanted to take Annie with him, he knew he could not afford it, and his departure late in October left her miserable. Then, on December 12, word arrived from London that after being sworn in as a member of Her Majesty's Privy Council, John had died suddenly at Windsor Castle.

Annie was devastated. Lady Aberdeen immediately rushed to her side and recorded the events of the next few days in her diary.

> I found her very brave & strong & quite natural & like herself — but at the same time utterly overwhelmed with the thought of being alone — "never to hear his voice again, never to hear him come at the door, never to hear him come up the stairs again — never, never — oh! I am afraid of the nights & I am afraid of the days & I am afraid of the years & if it were not for the children I should long to creep away in some corner & die." She spoke of how he had been her all in all — there was nothing else she cared for in life — society & other people were all indifferent to her unless she could through them do something to help him. And truly this was so — it [is] not an outburst of grief that makes her think like this now, but it has been evident that she just lived for him & that all the rest of the world were [sic] indifferent to her beside him — & this ever since she first knew him.

Despite her grief, Annie was able to discuss the political ramifications of John's death, and on the 13th she told Lady Aberdeen that she felt John Haggart, Minister of Railways and Canals, was the man best able to keep the Conservative Party together. She also said that if Sir Charles Tupper — a man John had greatly disliked — were chosen to succeed as prime minister she would consider it an insult to her husband's memory.

Later that day it was decided that Mackenzie Bowell should form a new government. But by then, Annie could no longer focus on politics: even though a doctor had given her a sleeping draught, she wanted, as Lady Aberdeen wrote, "to talk on about the past in a way which diverted her thoughts from the terrible present for a time at any rate."

Inevitably, however, the present obtruded, and when she learned that immediately after John's death Queen Victoria had sent for Sir Charles Tupper, then Canadian High Commissioner to London, and asked him to take charge of the body, she was beside herself. "To think," she cried, "that *he* should be in charge of my poor pet — that *he* should touch him & arrange things — *he* of all people." Her only consolation was the knowledge that the Queen herself had placed a wreath on the coffin before it left Windsor Castle.

After the funeral on January 3, Annie found herself face to face with the grim reality of her financial situation. John's estate was insufficient to meet her needs, and she became dependent upon a fund of $25,000 collected by national subscription. According to Lady Aberdeen, Annie's "first impulse was to . . . have nothing to do" with the money, but she later relented because of the children. She decided to live in Toronto where her two sons were studying law and by March was supervising the painting and papering of her new home, Derwent Lodge. On the 27th she had recovered sufficiently to tell Lady Aberdeen that the only way to deal with Ottawa society was to "feed them, feed them — nothing else will satisfy them."

In the months that followed, she continued to see Lady Aberdeen and on March 12, 1896 attended a tea party given by the Aberdeens in honor of Annie's eldest daughter, Babe. While Babe received guests in the drawing room, Annie took her place in the library and, as Lady Aberdeen recorded in her diary, "had quite a little levee which she enjoyed. She particularly appreciated Mme. Laurier coming and being very warm to her."

As she grew older, Annie lived much of her life in retirement in her home in Toronto. By early 1913 her health had begun to fail, and on April 9 she entered Toronto's General Hospital where an operation was performed the following day. Complications quickly developed and she died on April 10 at the age of sixty-seven.

HARRIET BOWELL

Almost as little is known about Harriet Bowell, wife of Canada's fifth prime minister, as is known about Mary Abbott, wife of Canada's third. Born in 1827 or 1828, she was the daughter of Jacob G. Moore of Belleville, Ontario. In December, 1847 she married Mackenzie Bowell, an Englishman who eventually rose from the position of printer's devil on the Belleville *Intelligencer* to that of publisher.

Although the Public Archives of Canada records that Harriet had at least five children, there are no direct references to her in the finding aid of the Mackenzie Bowell Papers. One of the few descriptions of her comes from the *Dominion Annual Register and Review of 1884*: "Mrs. Bowell . . . was a lady of an exceedingly kind and gently disposition, much given to charitable and religious works and warmly devoted to her husband and children."

If it is possible to judge a woman's life on the basis of her husband's personality, then Harriet's lot was scarcely enviable. Historians have denounced Bowell as a stupid, bigoted man who became prime minister almost by default following the death of Sir John Thompson.

The Montreal *Herald* described him as "an irascible old gentleman who despite his long political experience, works himself into a white heat on very slight provocation." Lady Aberdeen considered him "rather fussy and decidedly commonplace." In 1894 she could ill conceal her disgust with his inability to decide upon an inscription for the wreath the federal Cabinet had ordered for Thompson's funeral: "Only,"

54

Purported to be Harriet Bowell

he insisted, "do not put with kind regards."

Yet despite his faults, Bowell seems to have been a devoted husband. When Harriet died in Los Angeles, California, on April 2, 1884 while seeking a cure for her failing health, he was inconsolable. At her graveside, broken and worn, he bowed his head and murmured: "There goes my heart."

FRANCES TUPPER

In most successful marriages women learn quickly how to cope with their husbands. They stamp out highhandedness as soon as it appears and develop effective methods of punishing inattention. Women who do not live to regret it.

Such was the fate of Frances Tupper, wife of Canada's sixth prime minister, Sir Charles Tupper. In November, 1901, after fifty-five years of marriage, she was still the victim of her husband's autocracy. On the 21st she wrote to her friend, Mrs. D.A. McCaskill, confiding her latest grievance.

> There are regrets in every phase of life as the changes come, and it caused me a pang when my husband told me that he had offered our house for sale not that I cared so much for Ottawa but it was our home — and I had settled in it hoping never to move again.

At the time of her marriage in 1846, Frances was ill-prepared for dealing with a domineering husband. The only man to figure in her life before Charles was her father, Silas Morse, a native of Amherst, Nova Scotia and a man too tractable for his own good. When his obituary appeared in the Halifax *Morning Herald* on February 8, 1884, Morse was described as being

> at one time quite wealthy, but his kind disposition led him to assist many people with loans, by whom he met with considerable loss.

Generosity seems to have been a Morse family trait. Silas's father, Alpheus, was once called

Frances Tupper

. . . a very public-spirited citizen [who] gave a plot of land to the town of Amherst to build the first school-house on, as his father had done at Fort Lawrence.

Exactly when Silas, prothonotary for Cumberland County, incurred his first serious financial loss remains uncertain, but he and his wife, Elizabeth Stewart, seem to have lived well for many years. During the late 1830s and early 1840s they were able to send their daughter, Frances Amelia (who was born March 14, 1826), to Charlestown Academy in Massachusetts.

Details of Frances' early life are obscure, but it *is* known that after she completed her studies in Massachusetts she returned to Amherst where she met Charles Tupper, a young doctor with an interest in politics.

Charles recorded what happened next in his journal.

I made an offer of marriage to Miss Frances Morse, of Amherst. Having obtained the consent of her parents, she accepted my proposal and we were married on the 8th of October, 1846.

In a photograph taken shortly after her marriage, Frances' beauty is striking. Her heart-shaped face is framed by dark ringlets while her smoldering eyes and strong chin suggest a lively spirit: she looks like a woman more inclined to assert her will than submit it to that of her husband.

For a time at least, it appears that she *did* try to assert herself; but the ensuing arguments must have been bitter. Charles Tupper was not a man to give in. He has been described by one biographer as having a "dominating personality . . . [and] intense nervous energy which gave him quickness of movement and ceaseless mental activity." If he *was* a tyrant, Frances had one salvation: his patients were spread all over Cumberland County and he was frequently away from home.

Yet despite his faults, Charles was neither cruel nor ungenerous, and although he remained highhanded, he seems to have developed a cordial and caring relationship with Frances, especially in later years when they were uneasy if not together.

After their wedding, he bought Frances a new house and saw to it that materially she was in want of nothing. One thing he could not provide her with, however, was an antidote to gossip. Although he vigorously denied it, he was accused by the local quidnuncs of having had his medical training paid for by a wealthy woman in exchange for a promise of marriage. The rumor persisted for years — much to Charles' disgust — and eventually followed him to the floor of the provincial legislature.

Whether Frances was as disturbed by the gossip as Charles remains unclear. Certainly by July, 1847, she had more important matters to contend with: on the 23rd her daughter, Emma, was born. A second daughter, Lilly, followed two years later; but before Frances had fully recovered from the birth, disaster struck. While she was home alone with the children, a fire broke out in the stables and quickly spread to the house.

Charles, who had just set off on horseback to visit a patient, turned in his saddle to see smoke rising from what he at first thought was his neighbor's farm. After raising the alarm, he realized it was his own property, and he arrived home in time to remove a few pieces of furniture before the house was destroyed.

He eventually moved Frances and the children into a beautiful, three-storey home on fashionable Victoria Street, but their troubles were not yet over. In November Lilly died of what was diagnosed as "an attack of diarrhea caused by teething." After recovering from the loss, Frances and Charles decided to have more children, and their first son, James, born in 1851, was followed by a second, Charles, in 1855.

A few months before the birth of his second son, Charles indulged his interest in politics by running for the Conservative Party in the provincial election. Opposing him was Joseph Howe, one of the most respected politicians in Nova Scotian history.

Frances was incensed by Charles' plans, but her most fervent entreaties could not make him change his mind. Charles later told a friend: "One of my strongest opponents was my dear wife, who expressed the earnest hope that I would be defeated."

Then, as the campaign progressed, Frances had a change of heart. Sitting by an open window in a friend's house listening to her husband debate Howe, she realized how well suited his aggressive personality was to politics. "I do not want you to draw back now," she is reported to have said when the debate was over. "Well, I have made one very important convert today," Charles replied, "and I take it as an omen of success."

On May 22 he defeated Howe and began a forty-five year career in politics. A few days after the election, a letter arrived from James W. Johnstone, leader of the provincial Conservative Party. "I congratulate you," Johnstone told Tupper, "and sympathize with your wife in your triumph."

It was sympathy Frances would soon merit. For the next eight years her life revolved around her home and children (a fifth child was born in 1858 and a sixth in 1862) as Charles spent more and more time in Halifax, the provincial capital. Yet despite their frequent separations, Frances apparently encouraged his political ambition. According to one early Tupper biographer, it was to Fances that Charles

> ascribed much of the success of his public career from the day, as a young doctor, he entered the political lists and defeated the Hon. Joseph Howe. . .

One thing Frances did not encourage, however, was the excessive attention Charles paid to other women. It has been recorded that Sir John A. Macdonald was amused by Tupper's inability to leave women alone, and Hector Charlesworth, an early 20th century Canadian journalist, noted in *Candid Chronicles* that Tupper's "gallantry made him very popular with the ladies in private conversation." Whether his attentions were merely verbal remains open to speculation.

With Charles away so much, Frances gradually built her own empire. The children became dependent upon and devoted to her, and she developed an especial bond with Emma. In 1912 the Moncton *Daily Transcript* reported:

> In view of Sir Charles' busy life, the training of their children fell her lot. She was not only a devoted wife but also a tactful and successful mother in the social and religious training of her children. . .

Meanwhile, Charles was making a name for himself in Halifax. After his appointment to the Cabinet of Premier Johnstone, he turned over his practice in Amherst to his brother; then, to ensure his financial well being, established a new one in Halifax.

Finally, in 1863, he sold his property in Amherst and moved Frances and the children to a new home, Armdale, on the North West Arm. It was a house he and Frances would both become deeply attached to. In many ways, life in Halifax was little different for Frances than it had been in Amherst. The house and children still took up most of her time, and the only thing she had to adapt to was the increased social demands placed upon her by Charles' rise in the Conservative Party.

Then, in 1864, Charles' appointment as premier of Nova Scotia increased her social activity even more. Yet indications are that Frances did not enjoy serving as a political hostess. The Halifax *Herald* reported in 1912 that: "Lady Tupper has not been known as aspiring to leadership in society." Charles, however, thrived on politics and delighted in the attendant social activities.

Before long the provincial scene became too tame for him and he began to consider running federally. In 1867 he resigned as premier and was elected to the House of Commons as the member for Cumberland. Frances remained in Halifax while Charles attended the parliamentary sessions in Ottawa.

Two years later, in July, 1869, their daughter Emma married Captain D.R. Cameron of the Royal Artillery and so began a series of events that caused Frances great anxiety. In the fall, Cameron was appointed to the Council of the North-West Territories; but before he and Emma could settle into their new quarters at Pembina, Louis Riel seized Fort Garry and organized his own government. Within days Cameron had been arrested and released by the rebels. Conditions in the region were desperate, and he and Emma were forced to take shelter in a log cabin.

One morning while she was in the shack alone, Emma looked up to see an Indian in war paint standing in the doorway. The only thing she could think to do was feed him. As Charles later recorded

When all was consumed ... he had grown to a very large size. As he could not speak a word of French or English, he evinced his gratitude by patting his protuberant stomach with a guttural "Ha! ha! ha!" and left.

News of the insurrection spread quickly and according to Charles: "My poor wife was much alarmed when she learned the position of our only daughter. She told me I must go and bring her home."

That Charles went solely because Frances wanted him to appears unlikely. To be fair, he probably did share his wife's concern for Emma's safety, but he was too cunning a politician not to realize the political benefits such a trip could provide. Whatever the case, he left Halifax on December 3 and reached Pembina at 11 p.m. Christmas Eve. Emma's reaction upon seeing him amused him greatly: "When I went in, my daughter Emma sat up in bed and said, 'What did you come for?' " On January 3, after meeting with some of the rebel leaders, Charles secured safe passage out of the Territories for himself and the Camerons.

A few months later the announcement was made that Charles had been appointed to the Macdonald Cabinet. The demands on his time were now so great that he could no longer commute between Ottawa and Halifax, and he decided to rent (and later sell) his house in Halifax. Surprisingly, however, he did not immediately move Frances and the children to Ottawa. Instead, he took them to Highland Hill, a farm he had bought near St. Andrews, New Brunswick.

Much of what Frances thought and felt during her husband's long political career has not been entered into the public record. Fortunately, her contemporaries did not allow her to go totally unnoticed. In *Types of Canadian Women,* H.J. Morgan described her as "a woman universally loved and respected for her sweetness of disposition and high character."

Another contemporary, J.W. Longley, wrote of her attitude towards Charles' career.

> Throughout their long life together ... she stood by her husband rejoicing with him in victory, sustaining him in adversity, and was never by word or deed a clog on his

career.

But it was Frances' second son, Charles, who overheard and later recorded one of the most noteworthy compliments ever paid to her.

Two men, apparently old farmers, and both Liberals, were discussing Tupper. One said, though a strong Liberal he did not believe that Tupper was as bad as painted; the other in great surprise asked why; whereupon his friend told him he had been making inquiries about the family and understood that the sons were all respected and that the daughter was an exceptionally fine woman. He did not therefore believe that Tupper could be so bad a man with such children, nearly all of whom were of age! The other said that it was a fact that his children were in good standing and nothing could be said against them, but Tupper was as bad as he was said to be. The reason he gave for the children being so good was that Tupper married a remarkably fine woman!

After the resignation of the Conservative government in 1873, Charles and Frances lived in Toronto for several years. Then, in 1879, Charles was knighted by Queen Victoria. In a letter to Charles, Jr., Frances wrote:

You know your father does not care for these honours, and I am sure would have preferred for his own sake to remain plain Mr. Tupper to the end of his days, but there are other things to be taken into consideration in connection with it. I am sure he deserves the honour — he has merited any distinction Her Majesty could confer by his lifelong devotion to his country — his self-sacrifice. Of course, his wife and children may express this to each other.

Obviously Frances was proud of Charles. It is unfortunate that earlier letters are not available to give insight into her feelings about the demands his career made upon her and their life together. Yet whatever burden she had had to bear before, it was nothing compared with what she assumed after his appointment in 1884 as High Commissioner for Canada in England. As H.J. Morgan wrote

> During her husband's residence in London . . . Lady Tupper had many arduous and responsible social duties to fulfil in connection with his official position, which she discharged in a manner always creditable to herself, her husband and the Dominion.

In 1912 the Halifax *Herald* noted that although Frances was not by nature a social being, she was

> in the discharge of her duties as the wife of Canada's leading statesman and high commissioner in London for 13 years . . . ever a gracious and popular hostess; and not infrequently received special recognition of the successful manner in which she discharged her duties.

Perhaps her most important contribution to London society was the introduction of an annual reception and dinner in honor of Dominion Day. The celebration, attended by English dignitaries and Canadians visiting London, did much to boost Canada's prestige in Great Britain.

In December, 1895, Frances and Charles returned to Ottawa where five months later, following the resignation of Mackenzie Bowell, Charles was appointed prime minister. An election was called for June 23, but before either Charles or Frances could adapt to their new roles, the Conservative Party had been defeated. Sir Wilfrid Laurier was installed as prime minister and Charles took over as leader of the Opposition.

Meanwhile, Frances was preparing for their fiftieth wedding anniversary scheduled to be celebrated at their home in Ottawa in October. The Amherst *Daily News* of October 9 reported:

> The presents were a sight and numbered hundreds. They were of course all of gold. Their excellencies' [the governor general and his wife's] present was a small gold box of old English make and fine workmanship and inside the lid the following inscription was engraved: To Sir Charles and Lady Tupper on their golden wedding from the Earl and Countess of Aberdeen.

In a scene reminiscent of that staged by Alexander Mackenzie at his twenty-fifth anniversary party in 1878, Charles refused to accept the Aberdeen's gift because of a personal difference he had had with the governor general.

* * * * * * * * * *

Finally, in 1901, Charles retired from politics. It is at this point that the first real insight is gained into Frances' personal life: the correspondence she conducted between 1901 and 1906 with Mrs. D.A. McCaskill of Montreal has been preserved in the Public Archives of Nova Scotia. In the letter of November 21 in which Frances related Charles' arbitrary decision to sell the house in Ottawa she went on to say

> . . . I quite understand that it [Ottawa] would not be a restful home for my husband. I would always have preferred Montreal, but our income would not allow us to live there, and at our time of life we must be nearer or with our children.

She then added a comment that suggests she had not been as resigned to Charles' choice of a political career as some of her contemporaries believed.

> It was very disinterested of Mr. McCaskill to make such a gallant fight in support of the party, but he is only to be congratulated on being relieved of the great additional loss that sitting in Parliament would have involved. I am sure you are glad that he is free.

Three years later, on July 29, 1904, Frances wrote from Paris discussing their tour of Europe.

> . . . we regret not going to Mannheim when we were so near . . . I think the heat stupified us. We felt it very much after leaving Cologne until we reached Baden-Baden. . . I really ought not to have undertaken the journey . . .

In December she and Charles were in Vancouver spending Christmas with Charles, Jr. On the 30th she wrote:

We had a happy Xmas, our family . . . makes a party of 14 — and with four friends we sat down 18 to dinner on Monday. As Sunday was Xmas we spent it quietly . . . these grandchildren make us realize how old we are. . .

She then added a paragraph that suggests her own interest in politics.

It is dreadful to think of our defeat [in the 1904 federal general election] but far worse to realize what unscrupulous means were used to accomplish it, and how demoralizing for the country to have a Govt kept in power by the use of money . . .

On March 1, 1905, she made it clear that Charles was still up to his old trick of doing what he wanted when he wanted without regard for anyone else.

. . . we are sailing from Halifax in the "Bavarian" on the 7th of March. My husband only decided to go to England a few days ago.

Yet Charles could also be kind and caring. While in Rome (probably in April, 1905), Frances became ill, and in a letter to Mrs. McCaskill she wrote:

. . . I seem not to regain strength as I used to . . . The days have been very tiresome and the nights more so — but my husband has proved a good nurse — and has got up every night once or twice to give me a little nourishment.

Two months later she and Charles visited Emma at her home in England.

No words can tell you my delight to be in England once more. The rest and the quiet and loving care has [sic] made me quite myself again — and now that my husband is with me [he had been in a nursing home suffering from an unspecified illness] and steadily recovering I feel like a different being . . . I am quite convinced that so much travelling does not suit either my husband or me — and going to our children is all we ought to undertake . . . We are enjoying the quiet and the rest and the lovely gardens and lawn. The roses are in profusion as well as the other flowers and the air is lovely.

In another letter written while visiting Emma, Frances evinced her great attachment to her daughter.

. . . the past five months with our dear daughter has [sic] quite spoiled me for living without her. We have been surrounded with her children too and have been a happy party.

A few paragraphs later she revealed a strange shyness, made all the more remarkable by the fact that four years earlier she had told the McCaskills that nothing could "lessen our feelings of love and respect towards you both."

I have finished this little sachet — but I am not sure that I will have the courage to send it to you — if I do sent it will you ask Mr. McCaskill to accept it with my love.

One of her last letters deals with a car crash she was in while visiting England.

The motor accident was a great shock to both Emma and me, but she was thrown out and was for a short time unconscious — and we feared concussion of the brain — but she was mercifully spared and now only the scar over the left eye tells the tale. However, I am very nervous now about the horrid things, and it is in fear and trembling that I go in them.

Frances spent most of her remaining years in England and died there on May 11, 1912, at the age of eighty-six. Charles accompanied the body to Halifax and arranged for the funeral service to be held at Armdale, their former home on the North West Arm.

On May 28, 1912 the Moncton *Daily Transcript* reported:

[For] The funeral of Lady Tupper . . . the concourse of citizens who were present in carriages was one of the greatest seen in years . . . During the service Sir Charles sat at the head of the casket quite immoveable, except that occasionally the statesman displayed keen emotion, particularly during the brief remarks made by the archdeacon. His eye was bright and his manner alert, but he was evidently feeble.

After the funeral, Charles lived first with his son in Vancouver and then with his daughter in England. His diary for 1915 tells the story of his loneliness

Fri. Jan. 8   Dreamed I saw my Darling.
Wed. Jan. 20   Dreamt I saw my Darling.
Thus. Jan. 21   Dreamt that I was driving with my
                Darling from Amherst to River Phillip.
Thus. Sep. 14   Dreamt I saw my Darling. 63rd time.

More poignant still, is the tribute Charles paid to Frances while attending a celebration in honor of his eightieth birthday: "I married her with the bloom of Cumberland on her cheek, and that bloom is in my heart now." He died on October 30, 1915 at the age of ninety-four.

ZOË LAURIER

Zoë Laurier made a terrible mistake: she allowed another woman to become her husband's best friend. For twenty-five years she sat by helplessly as Emilie Lavergne, her intellectual superior, molded Wilfrid Laurier into one of the most successful politicians in Canadian history. Although Zoë could not meet the competition, she *did* outlast it and with her all-embracing charm became once again the most important person in Laurier's life.

Born in Montreal in 1842, Zoë Lafontaine was the daughter of Napoléon-Godefroi Lafontaine and his wife, Zoë Lavinge. Her father, a poor provider, was so frequently away from home that many people believed he was dead. No doubt there were times Mme. Lafontaine wished he were: without him, she might have found a husband capable of supporting her. As it was, she had to exploit her one accomplishment — her musical ability — by going from door to door giving piano lessons.

Over the years she developed a friendship with Dr. Séraphin Gauthier and his wife, Phoebe, parents of one of her students, and when her health failed she and Zoë went to live with the Gauthiers in their home on St-Louis Street. Eventually young Zoë, who had studied music at the Convent of the Sisters of the Sacred Heart in St. Vincent de Paul, took over her mother's teaching duties.

Then, Wilfrid Laurier, a law student at McGill University, was taken in by the Gauthiers as a boarder. At first he found Zoë shy and retiring and spent most of his free time

Zoë Laurier

alone in his room. As the weeks passed, however, he began sitting in the parlour with the Gauthiers listening to Zoë play the piano. Her hazel eyes and delicately chiseled mouth soon captured his attention, and when conversation revealed her great pragmatism and gentle humor, he felt his admiration grow.

Zoë, for her part, was equally aware of Laurier's presence. She found his good looks captivating, his bookish nature intriguing. Had it not been for his ominous cough, he would have seemed almost perfect.

Their courtship began slowly — so slowly that for months only the Gauthiers noted its progress. Instead of creating opportunities to talk to Zoë alone, Laurier discussed politics with the others while Zoë sat quietly in the background, her face often flushing in disagreement with what Laurier said.

Gradually Wilfrid's ignorance of the fine points of courtship frustrated him to the point that he became quiet and withdrawn, while Zoë, self possessed enough to give music lessons during the day, alternated between euphoria and despair as suppertime and Wilfrid's return from university drew near. The Gauthiers observed it all. Convinced the two made a perfect couple, they began leaving them alone together. Results quickly followed: one day the youngest Gauthier boy heard Wilfrid singing a love song as Zoë accompanied him on the piano.

Yet neither Zoë nor Wilfrid could really enjoy their blossoming friendship. While Zoë's mother lay upstairs dying, Wilfrid often sat in meditation convinced that he was suffering from consumption. Not all Dr. Gauthier's assurances to the contrary could ease his mind.

A year later he moved out of the Gauthier house, and a new suitor, Pierre Valois, a doctor from Pointe-Claire, began courting Zoë. From time to time Wilfrid called on the Gauthiers', but Valois' open and ardent wooing of Zoë dejected him and he saw little point in continuing his visits.

Then, after the death of her mother, Zoë stopped encouraging Valois and in the summer of 1866 allowed Wilfrid to take her for walks through the streets of Montreal. Their renewed courtship proceeded smoothly until one day in the fall Laurier collapsed at his desk after coughing up blood. Zoë visited him at his lodgings and once sat by his bedside holding his hand until Wilfrid, convinced that he was dying and that it was unfair to presume upon Zoë's affections, pulled it away. After that she wrote occasional letters, but their reserved tone indicated to Laurier that she was again focusing her attention on Pierre Valois.

It was a stressful time for both of them. Zoë loved Laurier and could not understand why she heard less and less from him. Meanwhile, Valois was pressing her to marry him. For months she could not decide what to do. Finally, in January, 1868, she accepted his proposal and they planned their wedding for May 23.

Wilfrid, by then living in Arthabaska with a Dr. Poisson, received the news with resignation. Although he had established a small law practice, he was still a convalescent with little to offer a prospective wife.

Zoë, however, did not see it that way. By March she had begun appearing at the breakfast table with eyes swollen from crying. Her unhappiness threw a pall over the entire household. Eventually Dr. Gauthier took her aside. When he asked what was wrong, she confessed that it was Laurier she loved, not Valois.

Laurier, it appears, knew nothing of her misery. Then, on May 12, as he was preparing for a case to be heard in court two days later, he received a telegram from Séraphin Gauthier. "Come at once," it said. "A matter of urgent importance." Laurier half suspected what Gauthier was up to and for a time considered staying where he was. By train time, however, he had changed his mind; and when he arrived in Montreal the following morning, he found Gauthier waiting for him on the platform.

As soon as they returned to St-Louis Street, Gauthier dragged Laurier into his office, ordered him to strip, then picked up his stethoscope. After the examination was over, he told Laurier that he had chronic bronchitis, not consumption, and that with care he could live to a ripe old age. "And you will certainly live longer than Zoë Lafontaine," he added sententiously, "if things go on like this." He then explained to Laurier where matters stood and suggested that a wedding take place that very day.

At first Wilfrid was furious with Gauthier for his presumption. Finally he met alone with Zoë in the library. Her surprise at finding him there made it clear to Wilfrid that she knew nothing of the doctor's interference. As the conversation progressed, however, she realized what Gauthier had done and her anger surpassed even Laurier's.

Within minutes their outrage and embarrassment had laid bare the feelings their reserve had hidden for so long, and when one of Gauthier's daughters walked by the library she saw Zoë and Wilfrid in each other's arms. Mme. Gauthier immediately began planning the wedding. A dispensation for the ceremony was obtained from the bishop's palace, and a marriage contract was signed providing Zoë with an annuity of $300 payable quarterly in the event of Wilfrid's death. She was also to retain control of her own possessions, which consisted of sixteen shares in a building society, her clothing, piano and household goods. At eight o'clock that evening they were married in a small brick church on Dorchester Street.

When the wedding party returned to the Gauthiers' house, the first person Zoë and Wilfrid saw was Pierre Valois. Zoë immediately let go of Wilfrid's arm and took Valois' hands in hers. In the excitement she had forgotten to send him a message. Valois smiled wanly, congratulated Laurier and drank a toast to the bride. His misery could only have matched his confusion an hour later when Zoë went with Laurier to the train station — not to leave with him on their honeymoon, but to see him off as he returned to Arthabaska to plead his case in court the following day.

Stranger things were yet to happen. When Zoë finally joined Wilfrid at the end of the week, he decided against finding a place of their own; instead, he wanted to stay in the house he shared with Dr. Poisson. The three best rooms were turned over to the newlyweds, and after Zoë had arranged them to her liking, she began receiving visits from her husband's friends. With Wilfrid beside her she felt little shyness.

Although she had been brought up in the city, she reveled in small-town living. She developed a passion for gardening and was soon growing her own flowers and vegetables. As the months passed her happiness grew. Her hospitable nature made her a popular hostess, and before long she and Wilfrid were so much in demand that one of the few ways they could be alone together was to pack a picnic basket and slip into the countryside beyond the Arthabaska town limits.

Their idyll was short-lived. In the fall Wilfrid's cough returned, convincing him that Dr. Gauthier's diagnosis of chronic bronchitis had been wrong. Zoë shared her husband's opinion. Before long they reached a tacit understanding that they would not risk passing on Wilfrid's respiratory problem by having children. Instead, they worked on developing close friendships with those around them — friendships they hoped would sustain them in the years to come.

As time passed, they showed little interest in finding a house of their own. Zoë believed that having Dr. Poisson under the same roof watching over Wilfrid's health was far more important than addressing their need for greater privacy. She and Wilfrid were comfortable and happy, and if their domestic arrangement was unusual, they didn't care.

Then, after the downfall of Macdonald's Conservative government in November, 1873, election fever swept the country. Laurier, who had maintained the interest he had developed in politics at McGill, grew restless and developed a cold which quickly brought on hemorrhaging. When a group of men arrived at the house while he was still recuperating and asked to see him, Zoë bristled. She knew what they wanted and told them her husband was not well. They persisted, and when Laurier heard the commotion, he told Zoë to let them in.

Ushering the men into the bedroom, Zoë tried in vain to catch her husband's eye. By the time the deputation left, Wilfrid had agreed to run for the Liberals, and on January 22, 1874, he was elected Member of Parliament for the riding of Drummond-Arthabaska.

In the months that followed, he and Zoë entertained more than ever before, and it soon became obvious that they had outgrown their rooms at Dr. Poisson's. To remedy the situation they bought seven acres of land on the outskirts of town, then built a spacious three-storey house of red brick. Within months of its completion, Zoë wished they could relive their early years with Dr. Poisson.

At a garden party in 1876, she and Wilfrid met Emilie Barthe, a woman just back from several years in Europe. Emilie's sophistication made her an object of awe in rural Arthabaska, and Wilfrid's partner, Joseph Lavergne, found her totally captivating. Their marriage in November, 1876 set the minds of many Arthabaskan wives at ease.

Certainly Emilie's appeal was not physical — her nose was hooked, her chin too long, her figure angular — but her poise and intelligence made her seem more attractive than she really was. Many people felt awkward around her. Zoë, who saw her frequently, considered her "a woman who would always prefer the drawing room to the garden."

Wilfrid agreed and suddenly found the drawing room held great attraction. With increasing frequency he strolled out of his office saying, "Joseph, if you will permit it, I am going to talk with your wife." Whether he wanted to permit it or not, Joseph was powerless to prevent it. Intimidated by Emilie's superior intellect, he had quickly resigned himself to paying her bills and accepting whatever attention she deigned to give him.

Zoë was equally self-effacing. There is nothing to indicate that she ever raised an objection to Wilfrid's growing intimacy with his partner's wife. Even when the local busy-bodies began speculating that Wilfrid and Emilie were lovers, Zoë remained silent. Whatever effect Mme. Lavergne was having on their marriage, the Lauriers managed to keep up appearances.

Then, during the election campaign of 1878, Wilfrid's opponent, a man by the name of Thibeault, told a crowd of reporters that "Laurier is disliked by the country . . . and he is disliked by his wife." The personal nature of the attack reduced his support, and he spent days explaining that he had been misquoted, that he had meant to say that Mme. Laurier disliked her husband's involvement in politics.

When the votes were counted on November 28, Wilfrid was reelected, and Zoë, who had been following the political scene for several years, resigned herself to the fact that he would spend the rest of his days in public office. The prospect did not please her. She had no political ambition for him whatsoever. It did, however, please Emilie Lavergne who had developed a great interest in Laurier's career. She recognized his strengths and decried his weaknesses. With her sophistication, she began molding the bucolic lawyer into an urbane statesman.

Years later she said: "When I bound myself in friendship to Laurier, I saw very quickly that this young deputy of the future was still in certain ways only the little greenhorn of St-Lin [his birthplace]. His wife was not the person who could teach him even those elements of etiquette which a man of the world should know, above all a political man destined by his talents to enter the highest circles. He did not even know the correct way to eat an orange at table. I made him understand that this lack of etiquette would hamper him among the English élite with whom he would be called upon to mingle in Ottawa. I taught him then to eat, to dress with taste, in a word, all that a gentleman should know."

Before long Wilfrid had outgrown the homeliness of Zoë and of Arthabaska. He felt more comfortable in the rarefied atmosphere of the House of Commons and of Ottawa drawing rooms. During his tête-à-têtes with Emilie, he discussed philosophy and literature — intellectual subjects in which Zoë had no interest.

When Emilie gave birth to a son in 1880, the gossips all but wore their tongues out; as the years passed, and the boy evinced a striking resemblance to Laurier, they winked at one another knowingly. Even then, Zoë and Lavergne behaved with remarkable stoicism. Zoë said nothing — at least nothing that has been recorded — while Lavergne shook his head and sighed. "What do you want me to do?" he asked his brother, Louis. "You say you don't believe the gossip, and neither do I. I have a good wife. Why humiliate her unjustly? She admires him as I admire him myself. All things considered I prefer to live in peace and let the people talk."

In Arthabaska the Lauriers continued to keep up appearances. They lived well and entertained often. When Wilfrid suffered one of his recurring attacks of bronchitis, Zoë nursed him faithfully; when he talked to Emilie of poets and philosophers, Zoë worked in the garden. Her earlier assessment of Emilie as a woman more suited to the drawing room than to the garden had proved only too accurate. To round out her days, Zoë played the piano and threw the house open to Wilfrid's nephews and nieces and the neighborhood children. Lawn parties became more and more frequent, and sometimes as she served cake to her young guests, Wilfrid entertained them with readings from history books.

Always, though, he was the consummate politician, and in 1887 his years of hard work paid off: he was named leader of the federal Liberal Party. Suddenly his interest in Emilie waned. Her unbounded ambition for him was now strangely irritating, and he soon began spending more time with Zoë. Although Zoë still disliked politics, she was shrewd enough to realize that if she wanted to maintain the new balance she would have to involve herself more in his career.

The following year she agreed to accompany him on a tour of Ontario. With her belief that most people are basically the same, she looked for the human being behind the public figure and soon was talking to politicians of their wives and families. Her ability to handle unfamiliar situations impressed Laurier, and some of their earlier closeness returned.

By 1891, however, Wilfrid was again deeply involved with Emilie. Zoë continued to appear with him socially, and on May 19, 1894 they attended a dinner party at Government House. Lady Aberdeen, who a month earlier had persuaded Zoë to serve with Lady Thompson as joint vice-president of the National Council of Women, was impressed with Zoë and in her diary wrote: "Mme. Laurier is shy, & prefers talking French — but is v. pleasant when one comes to talk to her — she looks sad [and] feels having no children."

Following the defeat of Sir Charles Tupper's Conservative government two years later, the governor general asked Laurier to form a new administration. Zoë partially closed their house in Arthabaska and moved with her husband to Ottawa. In August she attended the opening session of Parliament with Lady Aberdeen arrayed, as custom decreed, in full evening dress. Both women had hoped tradition could be disregarded so they would not have to wear evening clothes in broad daylight, and both had bristled at seeing their hopes dashed.

Eleven months later, Zoë accompanied Wilfrid to London for Queen Victoria's Diamond Jubilee. During their stay, Wilfrid was knighted by the Queen at Buckingham Palace. On the day of the Jubilee, Zoë, now Lady Laurier, rode by his side in a horse drawn carriage as the official procession made its way through the streets of London. Dressed in a gown of pearl gray silk, diamonds sparkling in her hair, she was as stately and regal as even Laurier could have wished.

For a time it appeared as though she again had won favor over Emilie. But Wilfrid soon needed his mentor more than ever; and to have her near, he set about finding a suitable position for Joseph in Ottawa. Finally he arranged a judgeship. When the Lavergnes arrived in the capital in September, 1897, Ottawa buzzed with gossip and speculation. Within weeks Emilie had established herself as the city's foremost political hostess. Zoë, still more comfortable in a small-town setting, could not hope to match her. After attending a dinner for Ottawa's élite, Lady Aberdeen noted Emilie's high profile in her diary: "Mr. Laurier took me in, His Excellency had Mme. Laurier and Mme. Lavergne."

No matter where Zoë turned, Emilie was there. Wilfrid could not enjoy a party unless she attended. Certainly Zoë's quiet charm was no match for Emilie's worldly sophistication. Even her afternoon card parties and evening musicales were eclipsed by Emilie's at-homes and tableaux vivants. Denied the place that was rightfully hers, Zoë found solace in her own admirers — two cats, two dogs and three cages of birds.

One of her few real friends in Ottawa was Lady Aberdeen. When the governor general decided in 1898 to leave Canada before his term expired, Zoë and Wilfrid twice entertained the vice regal couple privately. Lady Aberdeen recorded the first occasion in her diary.

> From Montreal we moved on Monday to Arthabaska, where we were met by Sir Wilfrid & Lady Laurier, who drove us over to their home . . . about three miles away, where we stayed from about 1 to 6 & had a most enjoyable quiet day . . . They gave us a nice simple lunch in the most perfect good taste alone with themselves — we photographed & were photographed — we walked up to the Church & then to the College . . .

In November she described the dinner the Lauriers held for them.

> . . . the suckling-pig, cooked in proper French Canadian fashion was the pièce de resistance, & very good it was. Then at the end A. [Lord Aberdeen] produced an old French loving cup copied from one of the time of Henri II with fleur-de-lis etc. & engraved with an inscription from us to Sir Wilfrid & Lady Laurier & "Oublier nous ne le pouvons" & having filled it with a splendid loving cup concoction it was passed around solemnly.

By 1901 Zoë's interest in politics had intensified greatly. She often sat in the visitors' gallery of the House of Commons listening to the debates and knitting. At about the same time, Wilfrid's relationship with Emilie started to cool permanently, and he had Lavergne transferred to Montreal.

Zoë immediately began a self-improvement program. Realizing that her halting English was a handicap in Ottawa, she worked until she became fluent, then found a dressmaker skilled in enhancing the appearance of sexagenarian women. She also involved herself in various charities and started addressing women's groups. Within weeks Ottawa gossips had noticed the change.

Her new passion for politics amazed Laurier. So did her increased sense of power. She began urging Cabinet ministers to find jobs for an ever growing number of would-be stenographers, clerks and post mistresses. As Laurier's biographer Joseph Schull said, she saw power and patronage as levers to be used.

Yet despite her new dynamism, Zoë would have preferred a different way of life.

> If we do not see each other as often as before [she wrote to a friend], it is because I belong to everyone and to no one in particular. I would rather be the wife of a simple *avocat* in Arthabaska. It was the best time of my life.

Eventually Zoë began taking an interest in the welfare of promising young men. One, William Lyon Mackenzie King, appeared especially gifted to her. By 1907 she was trying

— vainly — to push him into the arms of a wealthy widow from Brockville. Her intentions were good and her involvement in the affairs of others kept her from concentrating all the time on her loss of hearing and failing eyesight. By 1911 Wilfred had to guide her when they walked together and to caution her not to speak too loudly. Yet her mind was clear, and she still kept up to date on proceedings in the House of Commons.

When Wilfrid and his Liberal government were finally defeated on September 21, 1911, Zoë commiserated with her husband then told him that providence was giving him back to her. For Laurier the defeat was devastating. He did not expect to live much longer and he did not want to. Fears that he did not have enough money to meet their needs beset him constantly and Zoë's efforts to reassure him were not always successful.

In 1912 his spirits improved enough for him to decide they should go to Virginia for a two week vacation. Zoë, distressed by her infirmities, would have preferred to stay at home. "I fear to be an embarrassment," she told a friend. "In the old days I should not have borne to be parted from my husband, but today it is much changed."

Then, in 1919, Wilfrid suffered a series of strokes. As he lay dying, he held Zoë's hand in his. When the last attack struck, he squeezed her fingers and murmured, "C'est fini." It was all over.

Zoë was alone. In the months that followed, she concentrated chiefly on politics. Her position as honorary chairman of the women's committee of the Liberal Party was a source of great pride to her, and despite her advancing years, she attended the national convention.

In the fall of 1921 she caught a cold and her condition deterioriated rapidly. On the evening of October 31, she looked at her nephew, Robert Laurier, and said: "I think I am dying. I feel so tired, so tired that I would like to have a long, long rest, but I cannot sleep."

Later she whispered, "I think I will meet him soon."

"Whom will you meet?" Robert asked, but she did not reply.

After a while she asked how the campaign for the upcoming federal election was going. "Will the putting of

David Loughman and Dr. Bourque in the Progressive candidates hurt the Liberal chances in Montreal?"

She then asked questions about the electoral situation in various parts of the country and tried to persuade her nephew to honor a speaking engagement he had accepted for the evening. "Your uncle never refused to go anywhere when the Liberals in any district said his presence would help the Liberal cause, and you must not." She lapsed into a coma just after midnight and died a few hours later.

On November 7, William Lyon Mackenzie King, Zoë's protégé and the man who succeeded Laurier as leader of the Liberal Party, delivered a eulogy that subtly juxtaposed the public and private trials she had endured.

> Having regard to the many conflicts of bye-gone years in which she and Sir Wilfrid shared, there will always be something very beautiful as well as comforting in the thought that it was at a brief moment of political turmoil she should have been taken away from "the strife of tongues to where beyond those voices, there is peace."

LAURA BORDEN

Like Emilie Lavergne, Laura Borden was a woman at home in the drawing room. Like Zoë Laurier, she was also comfortable in the garden. Together, Laura's sophistication and homeyness should have made her the perfect prime minister's wife. Yet although most people who knew her found her charming, they also considered her rather austere. Isabel Meighen, wife of the future prime minister, Arthur Meighen, liked her very much but was always slightly intimidated by her.

The youngest daughter of Mr. and Mrs. Thomas H. Bond of Halifax, Laura, was born in 1862. Her father operated a successful hardware business on the corner of Duke and Upper Water Streets and owned a house in the city's south end. Although little is known of Laura's early life, it appears that she was brought up in a refined and socially active household. She played the organ, was interested in the theatre and enjoyed tennis, golf and water sports.

Her father's death sometime in the mid-1880s left the family in reduced circumstances, and Mrs. Borden began taking in boarders. Laura and her sisters helped with the domestic duties; but as a young woman in her twenties, intelligent and attractive, Laura wanted something more. To help fill her days, she practiced her music and occasionally played the organ at St. Paul's Anglican Church.

Then, one day, she was introduced to Robert Borden, a young lawyer seven years her senior who had recently gone into partnership with Charles Hibbert Tupper, son of Sir Charles Tupper. Details of their first meeting are unknown:

Laura Borden

perhaps she met him at one of the Church of England services they both attended; or perhaps she met him through her uncle, who commanded Borden's militia unit. Whatever the case, the two were immediately attracted to one another. Laura, dainty and petite, with dark hair, Roman nose and delicate chin, knew many of the business and professional people Robert knew. Her tastes and interests corresponded with his.

When Laura went to Antigonish for a summer vacation in 1886 their courtship began in earnest. Letters full of details of the lovers' daily activities flew back and forth. Gradually the letters developed a more serious tone; and when Laura returned to Halifax, she and Robert saw each other frequently.

For some reason, however, they were in no rush to get married. Whether they were uncertain of their feelings, or whether Robert wanted to build up his practice so that he could provide Laura with financial security, remains unknown. In any event, the courtship dragged on for three years; and they were not married until September 25, 1889.

Even then, they were not ready to settle into a conventional domestic routine. Instead of buying a house, which Robert could well have afforded, they rented rooms in the centre of the city and devoted their evenings to cultural activities, their vacations to travel. No doubt Laura had performed enough domestic drudgery at her mother's boarding house to last a lifetime. Now the hard work was behind her, and she looked forward to a life of ease. By Robert's own admission, he by then "had probably the largest practice in the Maritime Provinces," and financially they were in want of nothing. As he later recorded in his memoirs, their ambition was for him to continue practicing law "until some undefined date in the future when [he] might be selected for a position on the Bench . . ."

In the meantime, they concentrated on living well. A holiday in Europe in 1891 was followed by another in 1893, and in 1894 they bought Pinehurst, an elegant home on a large property overlooking the North West Arm. Nearby was Sir Charles Tupper's former estate, Armdale.

The following year they spent several weeks in England visiting London and the Lake District and frequently indulged their fondness for the theatre. Back in Halifax, they continued to embellish their life style. With Robert's annual income as high as $30,000 at a time when day laborers were lucky to make $300 a year, they were able to entertain lavishly and to take a prominent place in Halifax society. Over the years, they added to and improved the house until it was a virtual showplace. They both appreciated fine things and saw to it that they were surrounded by them.

In Laura's eyes there was only one drawback to life at Pinehurst — sunrise over the Arm. Robert was driven to transports of joy by the changing colors of the sky and wanted to share the beauty with her. Inexplicably, Laura did not consider daybreak a suitable time for a lady to arise, and she made it clear to Robert that she was not interested in watching the sunrise with him — sunset maybe, but not sunrise.

As the years passed, the Bordens remained childless. If they minded, they kept it to themselves. To provide herself with company during the day and perhaps to provide an outlet for whatever maternal instincts she had, Laura bought a St. Bernard named Taffy and a cat called Lady Jane. While the animals tolerated each other, they doted on Laura.

Whenever Robert spoke sharply to the dog or threatened to punish him, Taffy rushed to Laura's side and pressed up against her as though looking for protection. Once, when a cut on his neck festered, Laura sent for a veterinarian who cleaned the wound and dressed it. He had no sooner left, however, than Taffy tore off the bandages and reopened the cut. Laura immediately telephoned the animal hospital for advice. A disinterested voice on the other end told her that nothing more could be done: infection would set in and the dog would die; the best thing to do was chloroform him.

Infuriated by the lack of concern, Laura decided to cure Taffy herself. After making up bandages, she cleaned and dressed the wound, then wrapped Taffy's paws in cotton to prevent him from scratching his neck. For days she watched and waited. Then, when she changed the dressing, she noticed an improvement, and as the weeks passed, Taffy gradually recovered.

When he died years later while Robert and Laura were in Ottawa, word was sent to Robert at his office. As it was late afternoon by the time the message arrived, he decided not to break the news to Laura until the following morning. He knew she would be heartbroken, and he wanted to make sure she was well rested when he told her.

By 1896 Robert was at the pinnacle of his legal career. Then, in the spring, he was asked by Prime Minister Sir Charles Tupper, the father of his law partner, to run for the Conservatives in the upcoming federal election. Alone with Laura at Pinehurst, he faced a major decision — one it seems he tackled by himself. According to one Borden biographer, John English, Robert "chatted" with and "confided" in Laura, but did not "discuss" matters with her. If such was the case, their relationship must have been lacking in depth: it could not possibly have been one of equals; but rather one in which the dominant male looked upon the subservient female as a possession to be displayed, not a partner to be consulted.

In any event, after he "chatted" and "confided," he decided to accede to Tupper's request; but on the understanding that if he were elected he would serve for only one term, then return full time to his law practice. As it turned out, he *was* elected.

For Laura, then thirty-four, life would never be quite the same again. She was used to spending most of her days alone. She was even used to Robert being away overnight on business. But this was something entirely different. When Parliament was in session, he was away for weeks. When it was not, he spent all his time in his law office. The combination of the two roles left little time for rest and recreation and even less time for Laura.

Yet Laura adapted. She stayed at Pinehurst when Robert was in Ottawa and followed her regular routine of reading, gardening and occasionally seeing her friends. When she received letters from Robert complaining about life in Ottawa, she tried to cheer him. When he became lonely, she told him to come home "or I will have to come to you."

They both stayed where they were, however, and Robert learned to endure what he called the "miserable, irregular life" of a Member of Parliament. Later, when his health began to suffer, Laura relented and accompanied him to Ottawa for the parliamentary sessions. She enjoyed the social life of the capital and often sat in the visitors' gallery of the House of Commons listening to the debates.

87

As the years passed, it became obvious to her that Robert was not going to content himself with one term in Parliament. He was capable of more than serving as a backbencher; and after Tupper resigned as leader of the Conservative Party in 1901, Borden was chosen to succeed him.

The following year, Laura found herself pressed into service. Robert wanted to make a seven-week tour of the West, and he wanted Laura to accompany him. Because it was so important to him, she agreed. A delegation of Conservative M.P.s went along with them; but as Borden later said in his memoirs, they "were not always a happy 'family party' . . . jealousies developed . . . and the tension became so severe that one member absented himself and only returned because no notice was taken of his absence . . ."

The experience only reinforced Laura's desire to live her life peacefully at Pinehurst. Politics, with the attendant bickering and back stabbing, was abhorrent to her. Yet Robert's duties as leader of the party kept them in Ottawa a great deal of the time, and by 1903 he had begun to talk about moving there permanently. Their rooms at the Sherbrooke Hotel on Metcalfe Street were spacious and comfortable, but it was impossible to entertain in them properly.

Then, a fire at Pinehurst forced their hand. The damage was extensive, and they decided to look for a new house in Ottawa.

Before they could find anything suitable, however, Laura had second thoughts about uprooting herself completely. Although she enjoyed the social life of the capital, she preferred the more anonymous, more regulated life of a lawyer's wife. She also felt that if Robert returned to Halifax there would be fewer demands on his time. Prospects for his political future had dimmed somewhat in late 1905, and she believed the time was right for him to resign. For a while, Robert may even have agreed. Buried among the Borden Papers at the Public Archives of Canada is the following intriguing note:

> I hereby give my consent — in your
> getting out of politics and — quick.

Feb 4th 1906

Laura Borden

As the days passed, the note may have become lost in the jumble on Robert's desk. In the end, he persevered, and Laura saw her hopes dashed. Finally they began combing Ottawa for a new home. Nothing they saw measured up to Pinehurst, and they decided to build a place of their own. After buying a lot of land on Marlborough Avenue, they had an architect draw up the plans. Robert was about to hire a contractor when there was a sudden change of plan.

As he recorded in his memoirs, Laura had just returned from the wedding of her friend, Corinne Fitzpatrick, when she announced that "there was one house in Ottawa which, above all others, she would like to acquire." Robert approached Sir Charles Fitzpatrick, who was then renting the house, and asked if he intended to purchase it. After two months of deliberation, Fitzpatrick decided he did not. Borden then talked to the owner, Mrs. Hayter Reid, and his offer to purchase was accepted on April 25.

Glensmere, as the estate was called, overlooked the west bank of the Rideau River. The land fell sharply between the house and the water; and over the years, Laura and Robert enhanced the slope by planting trees, setting in rock gardens, and paving walkways. Laura did much of the lighter gardening herself and was especially proud of her roses and dahlias.

Yet the property *did* have its drawbacks. As Borden wrote: "On the west . . . a disused cemetery . . . was overgrown with shrubs and bushes; and in the evenings was sometimes the resort of very undesirable characters." Eventually Laura persuaded the Ottawa Improvement Commission to turn the land into a park modelled on one she had seen in England.

She also arranged for improvements to be carried out on the house; unfortunately, they ended up being more extensive than she had intended. As Robert wrote

> On the north the large dining-room was heated merely
> by a tiny radiator under each window-seat. We put in

three radiators; but even so one of the window-seat radiators froze and exploded during our first winter; and another went the same way during our second winter.

Laura, ever the gracious hostess, made Robert's life much easier. In a city where entertaining was important — often crucial — to a politician's survival, her social skills were invaluable. She played golf with the right people, attended women's meetings and entertained frequently. Ottawa society nodded in approval. In *Types of Canadian Women*, her contemporary, H.J. Morgan, described her as "an active-minded, amiable and talented woman, [who] has contributed much to her husband's success, both politically and socially, throughout the Dominion."

After they had been settled for several years, a flare-up in the House of Commons led Robert to consider retiring. He told Laura that his political career was over and that he was glad. She had hardly had time to take in the good news, however, when a delegation persuaded him to stay on. Six months later, the Liberals under Sir Wilfrid Laurier were driven from office; and Robert was sworn in as Canada's eighth prime minister.

In the summer of 1912, Laura accompanied him on a trip to England. The poise she had developed in the drawing room at Pinehurst proved more valuable than ever as they mingled with the nobility. Weekends with the Duke of Norfolk and the Marquess of Salisbury were followed by a Court Ball at Buckingham Palace.

Her public appearances drew large crowds, and she was frequently interviewed by the press. On July 10 she told a reporter for *The Standard* that domestic servants were the class most needed in Canada, followed by women with a little capital — provided that such women also had some initiative.

Three days later she told another reporter that she could see little difference between English and Canadian women "so far as types were concerned"; individuals, she conceded, did differ. She went on to say that although Canadian women were greatly interested in philanthropic work, she was "amazed at the amount of good work done by men and women in England for those not so fortunate. The
90

people in important positions appear to be always helping them." She believed it was essential that highly placed Canadians did the same thing; and in the years that followed, she took great interest in a number of charities, especially the Red Cross.

As the months passed, her popularity in Ottawa grew. She was sophisticated, but not pretentious, friendly, but not familiar. The thin layer of reserve she showed in public preserved her privacy and ensured that none but her intimates knew her well. Yet her reserve was not glacial. Neither was she artificial: if she had been, a sensitive, down-to-earth woman like Isabel Meighen would have been aware of it. Laura of the drawing room and Laura of the garden were quite simply two different woman.

In May, 1913, the Conservative members of the House of Commons acknowledged her contribution to the party's popularity by presenting her with an expensive automobile — an electric brougham. That fall she persuaded Robert, whose health had been poor for some time, to go to New York and then to Hot Springs, Virginia on a private vacation. They made a similar trip in April, 1914 and upon their return learned that Robert had been granted a knighthood.

When war broke out in August, Laura worked tirelessly for the Red Cross. As she had told reporters in London, she felt it was important for people in her position to help the less fortunate. By setting an example, she hoped to prompt other women into joining the war effort. Certainly the work was more rewarding then her usual routine of cutting ribbons and launching ships.

Within eighteen months the hectic pace had broken her health, and she developed pneumonia. While she was still recuperating, fire broke out in the House of Commons. Robert, who was in the building at the time, immediately worried that Laura would hear about the blaze before she knew he was safe. As he later recorded in his diary, he left the Commons, then went to the "Privy Council office where I immediately telephoned to Laura as I feared the shock to her in her weak and nervous condition."

The following year a general election returned Robert to office for another term. Five days after the results were in, he and Laura left again for Hot Springs. This time, because of the gruelling pace of her war work, Laura was as eager for the rest as Robert was. Unfortunately, they might just as well have stayed at home. As Robert recorded, "various troubles and difficulties on the railways" delayed their arrival until Christmas Day. The weather was mild when they got there, but, to their disgust, "an astonishing cold wave began on the same afternoon which resulted in a temperature rather like that of Ottawa." Telegrams arrived daily from various government departments, and Laura must have been both angry and disappointed to see their holiday turn out so disastrously.

In the new year, they returned to Ottawa, where Laura resumed both her war work and her social activities. Although she seems to have made a point of avoiding comment on political matters, she was not averse to speaking her mind on other issues. At the annual meeting of the I.O.D.E. in May, she objected to a motion to endow a chair in a Canadian university for the teaching of the history of the British Empire and to provide a centre for research into political and economic problems. Instead, she convinced the delegates that the money would be better used providing scholarships for the children of war veterans.

In 1919 Robert's health became a cause of concern to her, and by the end of the year he was on the verge of collapse. His doctor urged him to retire, and on December 14 Robert told Laura that he would step down in the summer. It was the news she had been awaiting for almost fourteen years. Robert's obvious relief with the decision pleased her, and one day she told him that he "was more cheerful and less worried" than he had been in a long time.

They decided to stay at Glensmere, and the years that followed were quiet and peaceful. In his memoirs, Robert gave a glimpse of their life together.

> Very often in the evenings we sit on the upper verandah, just above the sun-room, and watch with much interest the occasional games of very crude baseball played by boys and girls of from twelve to sixteen in Macdonald Park.

Laura maintained her interest in the Red Cross and spent much of her time helping the families of veterans. Often she provided clothing and tuition fees for the children of ex-soldiers.

In 1933 Robert, who had been at Echo Beach near Ottawa, accepted a lift back to the city in an airplane. When he arrived at Glensmere, he found that Laura had gone to a friend's house for lunch. His recollection of what happened next is a charming account of one of their more lighthearted moments together.

> I left a telephone message for her to call me at our house. When she telephoned . . . I told her I was at Echo Beach; and she expressed surprise that I could telephone from there. I explained that we had a new line installed of which she had not heard. She wanted to know why it was that she could call me at our house and get in touch with me at Echo Beach. I explained that I had arranged for an immediate connection as soon as she would call the house . . . She was most appreciative of my having taken the trouble to call from that distance . . . Later in the afternoon she reported the incident to a lady whose husband was also at Echo Beach. This lady was quite concerned that her husband had neglected to call her. When Laura reached home that evening I was waiting for her at the door; and she used graphic language to describe the 'grin' which pervaded my countenance. Very graphically also did she express her sensation; 'Of course I was glad to see him, but at the moment I could have killed him.'

Later that year, Robert celebrated his seventy-ninth birthday. During the celebration, Laura told him that he "should have a birthday not more than once in three years." She then added that "up to a certain period a woman is accustomed to understate her age; afterwards she acquires the habit of overstating it so that she induces admiring friends to say : "What a wonderful woman she is for her age!"

In 1936 Robert went to France to visit war graves and then to England. While he was away, Laura became ill but refused to allow anyone to notify Robert. In August the doctor diagnosed undulant fever. Although she was too weak to do anything herself, Laura arranged for more improvements to be carried out to the grounds. For months after Robert's return, she tired easily; and in November, Robert reported that she still had not fully regained her "accustomed strength and health."

The following year, Robert suffered a heart attack. A second, more serious attack followed three months later, and for weeks his condition was critical. Knowing he had promised to address the Canadian Club, Laura went to the meeting and delivered the speech herself. A few days later, Robert died at the age of eighty-two.

Laura stayed on at Glensmere, devoting her time to her books and garden. She died on September 7, 1940. Perhaps her most enduring epitaph was the tribute Robert paid to her in his memoirs.

> In 1889 I had become engaged to be married to Laura Bond . . . whose devotion and helpfulness during all the succeeding years have been the chief support of my life's labors.

ISABEL MEIGHEN

Women rarely find favor with their daughters' husbands. Those who do are remarkable indeed. Such a phenomenon is Isabel Meighen, who in 1985 was described by her son-in-law, Don Wright, as "a strikingly beautiful woman with a wonderful disposition that makes her beloved by all who come in contact with her."

The daughter of Charles and Lillian Cox, Isabel was born in Granby, Quebec, on April 18, 1883. After Charles' death in 1887, Lillian moved with Isabel to Birtle, Manitoba, where they lived for a time with relatives. A few years later, Lillian married W.H.H. Wood, the town's postmaster.

Although little has been recorded about Isabel's early life, it *is* known that that she received her teaching certificate from the Winnipeg Teachers' College, then returned to Birtle where she taught for several years.

In 1902, at the age of nineteen, she decided to spend part of her summer vacation in Winnipeg. Neither the shortage of hotel rooms in the city, nor the fact she had just had her foot trampled by a horse could deter her. An exposition was being held and Isabel was determined to take in as many of the exhibits as she could.

After renting a room in a private home, she set off to see the sights. A few days after her arrival, she discovered that several of her cousins were also attending the exposition — cousins who had somehow found accommodation at a downtown hotel. When they invited her to join them, Isabel accepted with alacrity. She loved socializing with people she

Isabel Meighen

knew and believed that she would have more fun as part of a group than she would alone. After receiving directions, she arrived at the hotel and went up to her cousins' room.

Meanwhile, Arthur Meighen, a law student and part-time real estate salesman from Portage La Prairie, was sitting in the lobby waiting to see a man interested in buying farm land. Time passed and the prospective client did not appear. Then a friend of Meighen's happened along and invited Arthur upstairs to meet some people from out of town. Meighen declined. He was not a man to put pleasure ahead of business. When his friend persisted, Arthur remained firm. Finally the friend shrugged and walked away. A few minutes later, he appeared with Isabel and her cousins and presented the group to Arthur.

For once, Meighen forgot about business. Isabel's beauty fascinated him. Her doelike eyes, graceful nose and delicately shaped lips were the most captivating he had ever seen. But there was more to her appeal than mere physical beauty. She had a charm and a quiet dignity that made her almost regal, while her lively spirit — so much at odds with Arthur's taciturnity — gave her an allure Meighen found irresistible.

Unfortunately he could find little to talk to her about. They could not even find common ground on the subject all Manitobans were discussing — the exposition. While Isabel found the fair thrilling, Arthur wasn't even interested in gaining admission to the grounds. As the others made small talk, Arthur grew desperate. Finally he drew Isabel aside and invited her to the theatre that night to see *Still Waters Run Deep*. Isabel accepted; and although neither of them knew it at the time, their courtship had begun.

Yet it had its obstacles. Arthur lived in Portage La Prairie one hundred and fifty miles from Birtle. Financially he was not in a position to support a wife. The demands of their careers made visits infrequent, but letters helped them sort out their feelings. When Arthur passed his bar exams in 1903, the future suddenly seemed brighter; and they planned their wedding for June 1, 1904. The ceremony was performed in the Anglican church at Birtle. After the reception, Arthur and Isabel left on a trip to New England and Eastern Canada.

A few weeks later, they settled down in Portage La Prairie, where Arthur had bought a frame house on Campbell Street. For Isabel the transition from schoolteacher to housewife must have been difficult. Instead of spending a full day in the classroom, she found herself with nothing to do but putter around the house. Her friends and family were six hours away by train; and to make matters worse, Arthur worked day and night.

Certainly she had her vexations. Arthur was notoriously absent-minded. His appearance, his meals, even his appointments were matters of complete indifference to him. As a housekeeper, Isabel tried to establish a sense of order; and she showed the same brisk efficiency and attention to detail that Arthur displayed as a lawyer. There were still more hours in the day, however, than she could fill preparing meals and ironing clothes.

Fortunately, she made friends easily. Her effervescent personality attracted people instantly and her sincerity encouraged lasting relationships. Moving in a circle of young married couples, she and Arthur did an increasing amount of entertaining. Yet while Isabel enjoyed showing off her home and making sure her guests were happy, Arthur longed for more quiet amusements. He did not share Isabel's sociability; and when he felt he had played host long enough, he would either go to bed or slip into the den and read. It appears that with time, he and Isabel came to accept each other's social behavior. He did not try to keep her to himself, and she did not fly into rages when he retreated from a party.

Then, in 1905, their social life was put on hold temporarily by the birth of their first son, Ted. (A second son, Max, followed in 1908, and a daughter, Lillian, in 1910.) Once, while Ted was a baby, Isabel persuaded Arthur to accompany her to a wedding. They left Ted with a neighbor, and after the ceremony went on to the reception and dance. At midnight, Arthur decided he had had enough. Isabel, who was having more fun than she had in a long time, wanted to stay; and they agreed that Arthur would pick up the baby and go home. Friends would drop Isabel off when the party was over. At 1:30 the dance ended and Isabel left with her companions in their car. When they pulled up in front of the house, she got out and hurried up the walkway. Waiting in the car to make sure everything was all right, her friends suddenly heard Isabel scream: "Where's Teddy!" Arthur had forgotten all about the baby and was in bed asleep.

By 1907 Arthur, as ambitious as he was absent-minded, had decided he wanted to do more than practice law; and he began to think about entering politics. Isabel was ambivalent. She was content with their present life, but she respected Arthur's abilities and apparently did not try to influence him one way or the other. When he decided to run for the Conservative Party in the federal election of 1908, she was proud; but she was also apprehensive about what would happen to her if he won. He wanted her to accompany him to Ottawa for the parliamentary sittings, and the idea of attending the receptions and parties appealed to her gregarious nature. But with the exception of her time at the Winnipeg Teachers' College, she had always lived in small towns; and she knew that life in Ottawa would be entirely different.

As it turned out, Arthur *was* elected. In the middle of January, 1909, he and Isabel bundled up the children and boarded the train for Ottawa. It was a journey they would make many times over the next few years and one that Isabel would always find tedious. As her daughter, Lillian, recently said, "Trains drove her crazy, but as there was no alternative, she learned to put up with them."

Once in Ottawa, they moved into the Alexandra Hotel on Bank Street; and Isabel began adapting to her new social life. Away from familiar surroundings, she was constantly afraid of doing something wrong, of committing some gaffe that would bring down public censure. She never did, however, and she kept her anxiety a closely guarded secret. Her social skills rivalled those of Lady Borden; and over the years, her grace and charm did much to compensate for her husband's more austere personality. She was a great asset to Arthur, and she contributed as much to his success as Laura Borden did to Robert's.

As time passed and Arthur's constituency demands and parliamentary duties grew, Isabel began to involve herself in his routine. Reminding him of appointments and commitments became one of her responsibilities. Of course, she could not be expected to do the impossible. She could only remind him of things he had remembered to tell her about in the first place. On one occasion, he forgot a dinner invitation he had received from Robert Borden. "Long ago," he explained in his letter of apology, "I adopted in self-defense a policy of advising my wife of my engagements and relying on her less treacherous memory but in this case I omitted that precaution."

If Isabel's inability to remind him of his social obligations was limited by his frequent failure to advise her of them, her ability to help him present a sartorially acceptable appearance was limited by his total disdain of fashion. His oldest, most disreputable clothes were invariably his favorite; and despite Isabel's most careful monitoring, he still managed to leave home occasionally in mismatched socks. One day he even appeared in the House of Commons in a pair of slippers. Another time, his haberdasher capitalized on Arthur's inattention to clothes and sold him a suit of spangled material that glistened in the light. When Isabel finally saw the monstrosity hanging in the closet, she drew the line. She could accept the fact that Arthur was too preoccupied to bother with mundane matters like dressing carefully, but she was not about to have him made the laughingstock of Parliament Hill.

As vexing as Arthur's absentmindedness was, Isabel had long since learned to accept it. Her main concern was his addiction to work. He was constantly busy. Constituency affairs often kept him away from home for days at a time. Occasionally, when he had an engagement that could be kept without being gone overnight, he hitched up the buggy and took Isabel with him. Once they took Ted along. It was the boy's first political meeting; and while Arthur addressed the crowd, Ted sat with his mother at the back of the room. Suddenly a dog burst through the half open door, barking furiously. Arthur paused as party workers got hold of the canine heckler and dragged him out. Later, when they were getting ready to go home, Isabel winked at Arthur and asked Ted what part of his father's speech he had liked best. She fought valiantly to maintain her composure as he replied: "The part where they put out the dog."

Unfortunately, such outings with Arthur were all too infrequent. Although he cared for his children, he was
100

too busy and too undemonstrative to show them his true feelings. As a result, Isabel was the one the children confided in and grew close to. Lillian remembers her mother as an understanding, fun-loving woman, capable of being firm when the occasion demanded, but always ready to play a game or to read a story.

Once, Isabel's strictness brought down her daughter's wrath. Lillian had not wanted to go to church with the rest of the family: when Isabel insisted, Lillian began sulking. She sulked all the way to church and when the first hymn was sung refused to stand. Isabel took a hymn book, forced it into Lillian's hand and motioned to her to get up. Lillian did so, but refused to sing.

Still seething over her mother's refusal to let her stay at home, she began plotting her revenge. As an idea took shape, she laughed out loud and was only brought under control by Isabel's rebuke, delivered in an undertone. When the next hymn was announced, Lillian sprang to her feet, opened her book and sang off key at the top of her voice. As people started looking over at the Meighen pew, she changed to the correct key and looked up at her mother, whose face was red with anger, as though imploring her to stop caterwauling. After they returned home, Lillian was punished for her behavior; but years later, Isabel admitted that once her initial irritation had worn off, she had found the episode extremely amusing.

Her down-to-earth, no nonsense style was not reserved for the children. When her mother-in-law was worrying in 1921 about whether she would be able to sleep on an upcoming trip to Scotland, Isabel declared: "Well, if you don't sleep you'll see just that much more!" The indisputable logic reassured Arthur's mother, and she went ahead with her plans.

Eventually Arthur and Isabel bought a home in Ottawa. The large brick house on Cooper Street was within walking distance of Parliament Hill, and Arthur frequently went home for a late lunch. With the children then in school, it was one of the few opportunities Isabel had to be alone with him.

Although she was fond of socializing, the endless round of obligatory entertaining must occasionally have palled on her. Arthur was moving up in the Conservative Party; and when they did not have guests for dinner, they usually had people in for the evening. Once, during a party they were giving, Isabel noticed that Arthur had gone into the den to work. After a while, one of the guests took her aside. "Won't we disturb Arthur with all this noise?" he asked. Isabel smiled, explained her husband's habit of disappearing and insisted that the party go on.

Over the years, Isabel had accepted the fact that Arthur's total absorption in politics left her to shoulder all the domestic responsibilities; and she was apparently content with her life. Like many politicians' wives, she had little interest in politics herself. Sitting with Arthur on the platform at Conservative rallies was usually the extent of her involvement. Occasionally, however, she *would* deliver a short speech — but only if Arthur could not be there to deliver it himself.

Her home was the centre of her universe, and home was where she wanted to be. Women's organizations held little appeal for her; and when she worked for the Red Cross during World War I, she always ensured that she left the meetings early enough to be home when the children arrived from school.

Then, in July, 1920, Robert Borden resigned as prime minister, and Arthur was chosen to succeed him. As wife of Canada's ninth prime minister, Isabel suddenly found herself in the national spotlight. She did not enjoy the new attention, but conducted herself with such poise and dignity that her reluctance to attend official functions was never noticed. According to Lillian, Isabel willingly accepted the demands placed upon her as wife of the prime minister. She was always ready to do anything she could to make Arthur's job easier. But even after twelve years in Ottawa, she still had an inferiority complex about being a small-town girl in the national capital. As Lillian put it: "She was always slightly frightened because of her lack of experience in big cities."

As had been the case ever since she arrived in Ottawa, Isabel's fears were groundless. In June, 1921, she accompanied Arthur to London and appeared with him on the 28th at a dinner party given by Lord and Lady Byng of Vimy. On the 29th, they lunched with the Prince of Wales at St. James's Palace and on July 4th attended a state dinner held by King

George and Queen Mary in honor of the King and Queen of the Belgians at Buckingham Palace. At each function, Isabel displayed her usual grace and charm; and any apprehension she felt was skillfully concealed.

A few months after their return to Canada, Arthur called an election for the end of the year. As the campaign got under way, Isabel bought a baby grand panio. It seemed a harmless enough thing to do. They could well afford it, and the fact it had been manufactured in the United States did not lessen her pleasure one iota.

A little while later, however, news of her purchase was published in *The Canadian Music Trades Journal.* The general manager of the Canadian Manufacturers' Association promptly wrote to Arthur explaining that Canadian piano makers felt somewhat aggrieved that none of their instruments had been deemed worthy of Isabel's consideration.

When more letters of protest arrived, Arthur dictated apologetic replies: he felt he had little choice; at the time, he was calling for tariffs on imported goods high enough to encourage the sale of Canadian goods in Canada. To Isabel, the whole matter must have seemed ridiculous. She had bought the instrument quite simply because it was the one she wanted. As it turned out, the piano did *not* become a campaign issue; and Isabel kept the instrument prominently displayed in her living room.

Arthur and his administration had more serious matters to deal with than alien pianos: their prospects for reelection were poor; and when the votes were counted, the government had been soundly defeated. A few years later, after a brief return to power in 1926, Arthur retired from public life and accepted an appointment as vice-president and general counsel of Canadian Securities Limited of Toronto. He and Isabel sold their house, packed up their belongings and moved to Walmer Road in Toronto.

In 1934 Prime Minister R.B. Bennett asked Arthur to represent Canada at the centenary celebrations being held in Australia's state of Victoria. With Isabel and Lillian as travelling companions, he sailed from Vancouver in early October. Calls at Honolulu, Suva, and Auckland thrilled Isabel. The people and scenery fascinated her; and when they arrived in Australia, she could not share Arthur's feeling that the three-week voyage had been tedious.

Nothing seemed to please Arthur. In Melbourne, the capital of Victoria and the centre of the centennial celebration, he was disgruntled to discover that there was more public interest in the Melbourne Cup Horse Race than there was in the centenary. While he stayed in his hotel room, Isabel and Lillian went to the track and enjoyed the race. In November, he returned to Canada alone, leaving Isabel and Lillian to linger and see as much as they could. As the years passed, Isabel's globe trotting instincts grew; and she continued travelling until she was almost ninety.

At home in Toronto, she devoted herself, as she always had, to her family and friends. Then, in 1953, Arthur became ill. Ménière's disease, an affliction of the middle ear, was diagnosed; and for two weeks, his condition was critical. Although he eventually rallied, he was never truly well again. After his death on August 4, 1960, Isabel spent a year with Lillian and her husband, Don Wright, then moved into an apartment of her own in central Toronto. Her life continued to revolve around her family and friends, and she spent much of her time sewing and knitting.

By 1978, she had become very frail, and although she continued to live in her own apartment, her activities were severly restricted. Today, she is confined to bed; and according to her grandson, Michael Meighen, "is no longer able to read or to watch television. While she sleeps most of the time, she is fortunately not in pain and on occasion is able to talk briefly."

The doyenne of Canadian prime ministers' wives, she celebrated her one hundred and second birthday on April 18, 1985.

Editor's note: Mrs. Meighen died in September, 1985 as this book was going to press.

JEANNE ST. LAURENT

Jeanne St. Laurent was the type of woman everyone would like to have for an aunt. Warm, caring, and totally without pretense, she could get to the heart of a problem in minutes. Her ability to make people feel that she had a personal interest in them made her the perfect partner for Louis St. Laurent, Canada's twelfth prime minister and the man known, because of his fondness for toddlers, as "Uncle Louis."

One of eight children, Jeanne was the daughter of Mr. and Mrs. Pierre-Ferdinand Renault of Beauce County, Quebec. She was born in 1887 and was raised in relative luxury. Her father, a prosperous merchant, owned a three-storey, turreted house in Beauceville and provided his children with the best of everything.

After attending the local school, Jeanne, plump, buxom, and with a firm chin, winning smile and sparkling eyes, was sent to the Ursuline Convent in Halifax, where she studied music and English and polished her social skills. Although her sisters had all shown musical ability, Jeanne's talent was sorely deficient; and when she returned to Beauceville, she had one goal in life — to find a good husband who could provide her with a fine home and children.

In 1905, she was invited to the graduation exercises at Laval University. The ceremony, considered one of the major events of the year, attracted the cream of Quebec society; and when it was announced that the Governor General Lord Grey and Lady Grey would be present, Jeanne decided to attend. As

Jeanne St. Laurent

she sat in the audience watching the graduates receive their diplomas, her eyes riveted on a young man just starting across the platform. Suddenly, as he walked by Lady Grey, the sleeve of his gown caught on her chair and pulled him up short. The audience was silent for a moment, then burst into a nervous titter as he struggled to extricate himself. Twisting in her seat, Jeanne felt a surge of compassion for the awkward, appealing, and soon freed stranger.

Back in Beauceville, she forgot all about the graduation. Then, in the summer of 1906, she went to a card party and found herself playing opposite Louis St. Laurent, the same man who had caught his sleeve on Lady Grey's chair. When the game was over, Louis immediately struck up a conversation with Jeanne and later asked if he could walk her home.

The next day, Jeanne told a confidante that she had found her "ideal." Not even the warning that Louis would be difficult to attract because of his devotion to books could deter her. He had already invited her to go walking again that evening, and Jeanne was prepared to let the future take its course. In the days that followed, however, she began to consider books a serious rival: almost a year was to pass before she heard from Louis again.

Finally, in the summer of 1907, a mutual friend arranged for them to meet, first at a picnic and then at a bazaar. On the second occasion, Jeanne was serving dinner to visiting dignitaries; but she found a moment to suggest to Louis, who by then was working for a law firm in Quebec City, that he go to her home and introduce himself to her mother.

After he returned to Quebec City a few days later, Louis began writing to Jeanne. The regularity of the correspondence concerned Jeanne's father; and seeing one sealed letter too many, he decreed that whatever the two had to say in future should be said openly — on post cards. Louis and Jeanne heeded the order; and despite the lack of privacy, their courtship flourished.

Still not satisfied that Louis was entirely honorable, Renault seized the first opportunity to go to Quebec City and ask him what his intentions were. Stunned by the older man's directness, Louis admitted that he was contemplating

107

marriage. That was all Renault wanted to hear, and plans were quickly made for Jeanne to meet Louis' family.

Unfortunately, it did not promise to be the most cordial of visits. The St. Laurent sisters did not think anyone was good enough for Louis, and they looked down on people from Beauce County because of their distinctive accent. In the end, however, Jeanne won the day. Her background and refinement measured up, and she bore no trace of the Beauce County twang.

Having collected the St. Laurent seal of approval, she and Louis announced their engagement. The only remaining problem was the prospective bridegroom's income. Fifty dollars a month would not support a woman accustomed to fine clothes and a houseful of servants, and Louis wanted to provide Jeanne with as many luxuries as he could. Finally, he went into partnership with a well-established lawyer and declared that the last obstacle had been cleared away.

The marriage took place at the Renault home in Beauceville on May 19, 1908. Before leaving on their wedding trip to Niagara Falls, Jeanne and Louis went down to the basement and burned the breadboxful of post cards they had exchanged during their courtship. On May 26, they went to Quebec City, where they hoped to remain permanently. They spent the first few weeks in a boarding house, then moved into a well-furnished, eight-room flat on rue St-Jean. From the beginning, they had a maid.

At least for the first year, Jeanne must have been bored. Her social life was, by choice, restricted to visits from family and a few close friends. She had no particular hobbies to occupy her time; and with a maid, she could not even putter around the house. Louis worked from eight in the morning until six in the evening, and Jeanne saw him only briefly at lunch. After dinner, she sat quietly while he worked for several more hours. When he was finally finished, she would get out a deck of cards and play with him until bedtime.

Then, in March, 1909, the first of her five children was born. Because she disliked hospitals, she gave birth to the first three in an improvised delivery room at home. Jeanne enjoyed raising her children and devoted all her energy to developing as close-knit a family as possible. Over the years, her efforts proved successful.

Eventually, as they became more prosperous, she and Louis began to talk of finding a house of their own. In 1912, they bought two adjoining lots on the Grand Allée, near the Plains of Abraham, and in 1913 built a three-storey, fifteen-room house of white brick.

Four years later, Louis became ill. His doctors suspected tuberculosis and prescribed rest and fresh air. Before long, Louis was talking of giving up his practice and becoming a farmer. The idea must have seemed ludicrous to Jeanne: no one knew better than she did how unhappy he would be performing the same chores day after day. To her relief, he abandoned the idea and, after spending the summer in the country, returned to his office, completely cured.

In 1920, he was called upon to plead his first case before the Judicial Committee of the British Privy Council, then Canada's final court of appeal. Jeanne accompanied him to London, but was so seasick and missed her home and children so much, that when he returned to England in future years, she usually stayed in Quebec City. Nothing was more important to her than her family. It must have been a source of tremendous satisfaction to her that Louis, unlike many men, spent most of his leisure time at home. Their life was happy and well-ordered; and as the children grew up, the addition of grandchildren only increased Jeanne's contentment.

Then, on Thursday, December 4, 1941, her way of life changed abruptly. At 6 p.m., she was in the kitchen supervising the cook and maid as they prepared to serve dinner. Two of her sons, Renault and Jean-Paul, were in the dining room with their father. When the roast had been taken in and the vegetable dishes placed on the table, the family sat down. They were almost through the first course when the telephone rang. It was Prime Minister Mackenzie King asking Louis to leave for Ottawa at once. Although King did not say what he wanted, both Louis and Jeanne suspected what was afoot. Ernest Lapointe, Minister of Justice and King's Quebec lieutenant, had died eight days earlier, and the prime minister needed someone who could hold the support of French Canadians. Louis' prominence in Quebec legal circles made him a prime candidate.

Jeanne did not try to conceal her dismay. She was fifty-four, Louis fifty-nine. Suddenly and without warning, their entire way of life had been threatened; and she was not going to let it be destroyed — not without a fight. Before the dishes had been cleared away, she told Louis that he had enough to look after as head of the family and head of his law firm. His place was in Quebec City, not Ottawa. When those arguments failed to dissuade him from going, she became more acerbic and pointed out that he knew absolutely nothing about politics and that there were people far better qualified than he was to replace Lapointe.

Louis listened calmly. He was content with his life, but he also felt a sense of duty. Canada was at war, and he would do anything he could to help his country. Yet by the time he was ready to leave for Ottawa, he was convinced that Jeanne was right. "I don't know for sure why the prime minister wants to see me," he told her, "but if it is to enter politics, I'll tell him that at almost sixty years of age, it's too late." Jeanne nodded. Louis' intentions were good, but she must have suspected that the matter was not settled.

As it turned out, King *did* want Louis to join his Cabinet; and in the end, Louis agreed. The following year he ran successfully for the Liberals in the riding of Quebec-East. For Jeanne, the new order necessitated some painful adjustments. She refused to leave their Grande Allée home for more than a few days at a time. When she did join Louis in his two-room suite at the Roxborough apartment-hotel in Ottawa, she took with her a refreshing breath of home. Armed with an electric kettle and hot plate, she prepared breakfast on a bedside table: from under the bed, she produced a basket of homemade jams.

Because Jeanne's visits were so few and so brief, Louis usually made the seven-hour train trip home to Quebec City every Friday. His arrival was the high point of Jeanne's week. Sunday nights, however, were not as pleasant; and she and Louis grew to dread them. Goodbye became only harder to say. During a particularly wrenching farewell, one of their daughters told them that if they were going to let the anguish of Sunday night ruin the little time they had together, Louis would have to stay in Ottawa until his term expired!

When he had agreed to join the Cabinet, Louis had done so on the understanding that he would return to private life as soon as the war was over. In 1946, however, he faced a major decision: Mackenzie King wanted him to stay on, while Jeanne wanted him to return to Quebec City and resume the practice of law. Her dislike of politics was not Jeanne's only reason for wanting Louis to come home. Their financial affairs had deteriorated during his five years in Ottawa; and with Louis nearing retirement, it was time to recoup their losses.

As he had been in 1941, Louis was determined to turn the prime minister down. Yet when he met with King, he bowed to the prime minister's power of persuasion. Jeanne had not forgotten the way Louis had given in five years earlier; and when he called her from Ottawa, she immediately asked what had happened. Her reply to Louis' announcement that he would soon be sworn in as Minister for External Affairs has not been put on public record. If Jeanne was dismayed by Louis' decision, she was in for even greater upset.

When King resigned as prime minister and leader of the Liberal party in 1948, he felt there was only one man worthy of succeeding him — Louis St. Laurent. The opportunity to serve as prime minister was more than Louis could resist. Although Jeanne continued to long for his return to private life, she accepted the fact that Louis had a rendezvous with destiny.

At a party gathering in late autumn, she stood on the sidelines while Louis delivered his speech accepting the leadership. As he neared the end of the address, Jeanne was ushered onto the platform and was seated beside Mackenzie King. When Louis turned around and saw her, his eyes misted; and he bent down and kissed her. The crowd applauded wildly, and Jeanne was led to the microphone. In a subdued voice, she thanked the delegates for the honor and trust they had bestowed upon her husband. The crowd responded enthusiastically. Louis was the first prime minister in almost thirty years to have a wife. (Both R.B. Bennett and Mackenzie King had been bachelors.) Once again there would be a woman to lend grace and dignity to the prime minister's official social duties.

Yet despite Louis' new position, Jeanne continued to spend most of her time in Quebec City. She went to Ottawa whenever the occasion demanded; and although she was reluctant to take part in public functions, she shared Isabel Meighen's ability to hide that reluctance.

During the two-week parliamentary Easter recess of 1949, she accompanied Louis on an election tour of the western provinces, then, in the months that followed, joined him as he visited a different constituency in Ontario and Quebec every weekend. One event during the campaign suggests that despite Jeanne's dislike of politics, she not only followed the fortunes of the Liberal Party, but also had good political instincts. When Louis was grappling with a personnel change, Jeanne heard him mention that he was considering promoting Paul-Emile Côté, a parliamentary assistant. She considered for a moment, then asked: "Why not the other Côté?" Alcide Côté, a private member, was both affable and popular; and Jeanne felt his personality would win support for the Liberal Party. Louis agreed, and Alcide Côté's promotion was announced.

On election night, as the polls closed across the country, Jeanne spoke with a reporter. "If my husband is elected," she said, "I won't sleep very much. If he is defeated, I will sleep very well. Then I will go back home." As it turned out, she had a wakeful night. Louis and his Liberal Party were returned with a large majority.

Before the new parliamentary session began, Jeanne persuaded Louis to take their first real holiday together since 1941. With their children and grandchildren, they went to Kent Lodge, near Bathurst, New Brunswick, where they relaxed completely. One day while they were there, Louis told Jeanne that his old bathrobe was out of style and asked her to shorten it. Jeanne, in mock indignation over what she called his desire to show off his legs to the bathing beauties, balked and could only be cajoled into making a modest adjustment. Such carefree moments helped make the summer one of the happiest they had ever shared.

By August, however, the idyll was over. Louis returned to his Roxborough apartment in Ottawa and was soon busy with affairs of state. Meanwhile, efforts were under way to transform a large house at 24 Sussex Drive into an official prime ministerial residence. There was just one problem: the St. Laurents did not want a house in Ottawa. Louis was satisfied with his apartment, and Jeanne was as attached as ever to their home in Quebec City. The bureaucrats paid no attention; and when they had made all the necessary arrangements, they offered the house to the prime minister. In the end, Jeanne and Louis agreed to move in: but Jeanne did not try to hide her reluctance. "My home," she told a reporter, "is here in Quebec City." To reinforce her position, she refused to close up their house on the Grande Allée.

Despite the fact their wishes had been ignored, she and Louis had one consolation: they were together again, and they were going to make the most of it. Whenever it was possible, Jeanne travelled with Louis — usually in the private railway car reserved for the prime minister. The comfort and privacy of the car allowed them to salvage a little bit of each day for themselves when they were away on official business.

One thing Jeanne would not do, however, was travel by plane. She told Louis that she would not fly until she sprouted wings of her own. Even when they were invited to attend Queen Elizabeth's coronation in London in 1953, she refused to yield; and they made arrangements to sail on the luxury liner, *Queen Elizabeth.*

After their arrival in London on May 26, they faced a hectic two-week schedule of public functions that saw them whisked back and forth across England. They attended a garden party at Buckingham Palace, travelled to Oxford, met with the Churchills, and, on June 2, took part in the official coronation procession from Buckingham Palace to Westminster Abbey.

Although the Queen of the Tonga Islands defied the rain and lowered the top of her carriage so the people could admire her, Jeanne did not follow suit. Apparently she felt that the public would find nothing appealing in a woman sodden by the elements. She entered the Abbey warm and dry and took her seat directly in front of Louis, who with three other Commonwealth prime ministers, flanked Queen Elizabeth. After attending a prime ministers' conference a few days later, Louis flew back to Canada while Jeanne returned by ship the following week.

In 1954, Louis left on a six-week world tour. When faced with the choice of remaining alone on solid ground or joining her husband in an air force jet, Jeanne decided upon the former. She was lonely while he was away; and when he returned on March 9, she was at the airport to meet him. Louis,

113

the first off the plane, rushed up to her, placed a garland of flowers around her neck and, in a rare public demonstration of affection, kissed her.

Through the years, Jeanne had made no secret of her dislike of public life. Everyone in the St. Laurent family thus assumed that when her son, Jean-Paul, announced his intention of entering politics, Jeanne would be bitterly opposed. They were in for a surprise. Jean-Paul had always been Jeanne's favorite; and when he asked her to support him, she found it impossible to refuse. Louis, however, did not hesitate to voice his objection. In his eyes, Jean-Paul was capitalizing on the St. Laurent name. Jeanne quickly took Louis to task; and in the end, Jean-Paul sought and won the Liberal nomination.

In February, 1957, Louis celebrated his seventy-fifth birthday. At a party held for him in Quebec City by the Liberal Party, he looked on as a huge cake was placed in front of him. Failing to put out all seventy-five candles in a single puff, he leaned closer to the cake and blew more vigorously. When he straightened up, his dinner jacket was smeared with frosting. Instinctively, Jeanne grabbed a napkin and began dabbing at his lapels. As she scolded him gently for being so clumsy, the audience applauded in delight.

A few months later, the Liberals lost the federal election; and Louis was replaced as prime minister by John Diefenbaker. The St. Laurents did not move into Stornoway, the house used since 1950 as the residence of the leader of the Opposition, but returned to their own home on the Grande Allée. Although Jeanne must have sympathized with Louis in his fall from power, she was glad to return to a less demanding way of life.

All that remained was for Louis to resign as leader of the Liberal Party. For several weeks he could not bring himself to do it. Then, in September, he called for Lester Pearson, a prominent party member, and asked him to help draft a letter of resignation. Jeanne seemed relieved to see Pearson and served a lavish supper. When Louis signed the letter the next morning, she was positively radiant. Bustling around the house with a smile she could not hide, she planned a roast beef dinner. The strain was over, and she looked forward to a return to the happy family life they had enjoyed before Louis entered politics.

In the years that followed, they received frequent visits from their children and grandchildren and spent their evenings playing cards and watching television. Gradually, Jeanne's health began to fail; and she died in the house she had loved so much on November 14, 1966. Louis remained active until a fall in 1968 left him with a broken hip. He died on July 25, 1973, at the age of ninety-one.

OLIVE DIEFENBAKER

When Olive Freeman first met John Diefenbaker at a church gathering in 1917, she was a fifteen-year-old schoolgirl still in pigtails; he was a twenty-two-year-old law student just back from an officer training course in England. At first the age difference did not matter. Olive was mature for her years, and her quick repartee made her more than a match for John in their church group debates.

Then, on the day he finally asked her for a date, Olive confessed her age. Realizing the problems in going out with a girl so young, John turned his attention elsewhere. Decades were to pass before the two met again.

Olive Evangeline Freeman, one of five children, was born in Roland, Manitoba, in 1902. Her father, the Reverend Charles B. Freeman, grew up in Canning, Nova Scotia, across the road from his future wife, Angie Eaton. Two of Freeman's ancestors landed at Plymouth Rock on the *Mayflower* in 1620 while other forebears fought with Wolfe at Quebec before immigrating to Nova Scotia during the American Revolution.

In 1891 Charles graduated from Acadia University in Wolfville, Nova Scotia, and entered the Baptist ministry. A gentle man, he raised his three sons and two daughters in a refined, middle-class home.

As an adult, Olive attributed her self-possession to the lessons she had learned as a child. "I am accustomed to public scrutiny," she told a friend after John had become prime minister. "I was brought up in a parsonage. Whenever we got a new hat or dress people were sure to talk about it."

Olive Diefenbaker

The barbs of public criticism drew the Freeman family together. According to Olive, her mother had a pride and dignity that prevented her from "pulling a poor mouth" even when times were bad. Her father possessed equal character and rarely missed an opportunity to teach his children the value of self-reliance.

In 1957 Olive recalled one of his most successful lessons. "One day I took a problem to my father and asked for his advice. He simply restated the problem and smiled kindly. 'I know that,' I replied, 'but what shall I do?' Again he outlined the problem. On the third time around I threw up my arms in exasperation. 'Oh, for goodness' sake!' I said, then I made up my own mind. It was an important lesson and one that has borne lifelong results. I know now what he was doing."

As a student, Olive fared well. Intelligent and curious, she applied herself to her studies and at an early age decided to become a teacher. It was in the fall of 1917, while she was making definite plans for her future, that she met John Diefenbaker in the basement of her father's Saskatoon church.

Not long before he died, John romanticized and no doubt fictionalized the story of their first meeting. As he remembered it, they had just gone their separate ways when he wrote and asked her to marry him. The letter was lost in the mail, and Olive did not receive it until ten years later. Taking her silence as rejection, John returned to his studies while Olive enrolled at the University of Saskatchewan in Saskatoon.

Later she moved with her parents to Brandon and attended Brandon College before going on to Hamilton where she received her Bachelor of Arts Degree from McMaster University. A year later she earned a high school teaching diploma at the Ontario College of Education and taught in Huntsville and Guelph until 1932. In the meantime, John had graduated with his law degree and in 1929 had married Edna Brower, an elementary school teacher.

By 1930 Olive, a vibrant woman with striking features, boundless energy and a dynamic personality, was professionally well established. She had the ability to listen and to communicate, and her sensitivity gave students the self-confidence they needed. After several years of practical experience she began to believe that teachers should understand their students as well as their subjects. Bursting with self-assurance, she envisaged a bright future for both herself and the education system in Ontario.

Then, in 1933, she married Harry Palmer, a lawyer and cellist she had met in Guelph. Although she wanted to continue teaching, she bowed to the convention that required married women to stay at home and in 1934 gave birth to her only child, a daughter, Carolyn. Two years later her husband died and Olive returned to work.

Accepting a teaching position first in Arthur, Ontario and later in Owen Sound, she devoted the next seventeen years to her daughter and her career. In the classroom her interest inspired her students to achieve while her skill as a basketball coach earned their admiration.

Once she arranged for an exceptionally bright third year boy to take fifth year history. Within weeks he was the leader of his class. Later she suggested that he start a speaking club. "I don't like to push myself," he complained. "That's just it," she replied, "you don't *have* to push yourself." In his final year he was head of the entire student body.

With her progressive approach to education, Olive took a special counselling course at McMaster and became one of Ontario's pioneers in educational guidance. In 1945 she was appointed Assistant Director of Vocational Guidance for the Province of Ontario and soon began to appear on the lecture circuit in both Canada and the United States. By showing teachers how to keep students from dropping out and how to help them choose and train for suitable careers, she hoped to improve the standard of education.

The demands on her time were enormous and occasionally her energy ebbed. But regardless of the pressure, she spent all the time with Carolyn she could. Often she would drive fifty or sixty miles from a speaking engagement just to spend the evening at home.

Once she was called upon to deal with a school principal notorious for his opposition to the guidance system. Blazing into his office, Olive furrowed her brow and wagged her finger. "Now, look here," she exclaimed with mock severity, "you're going to listen to me!" They both laughed, then sat down and worked out an agreement establishing a new guidance class.

119

Although she little realized it at the time, she was gaining valuable experience for her future role as wife of Canada's thirteenth prime minister. Saying the right thing at the right time and knowing when to bite her tongue were vital to her success both as John's wife and as Assistant Director of Vocational Guidance.

When asked to assume the directorship in 1953, Olive quietly declined. For several months she had been secretly seeing John Diefenbaker, by then a prominent lawyer and politician, whose first wife had died in 1951. Even the few close friends who knew about the relationship saw no hope for it. One couple who had invited Olive and John to their home for a long weekend dismissed the whole thing. "There's nothing to it," they said. "They're not even close friends." Olive and John knew better, however, and on December 8, 1953, they were married in Toronto.

For John the marriage marked a major turning point. In the months following the death of his first wife, he had grown gloomy and sullen; after he had renewed his acquaintance with Olive his spirit had returned, and by the time they had been married a few months he was again a vital political force.

The marriage also marked a turning point for Olive. Until 1953 — with the exception of the three years she had been married to Harry Palmer — her adult life had revolved around her daughter and her career. Gradually Carolyn had lessened her dependence, but the guidance department had not. With one stroke of her pen, Olive had resigned her position and put both the demands and the satisfactions of her career behind her. The sacrifice was made willingly. But Olive was no self-effacing milquetoast. In order to fulfill herself, she had to transfer her conviction and vitality to another cause. That cause became the political career of John Diefenbaker.

"The whole direction of my life," she once said, "is that I am John's wife." Even her interest in painting, ballet and classical music took a back seat to John. "My recreation is what John likes and he likes none of these." By today's standards such devotion sounds vacuous, but if we recognize that as a wife she wielded enormous power, it assumes new meaning.

The extent of her influence first became clear in 1956 when she urged John to attack the Liberal government for undermining the power and prerogative of Parliament. Although some Conservative strategists disagreed with Olive's political instincts, John followed her advice and scored a resounding political triumph.

That same year he won the leadership of the federal Progressive Conservative Party. When told at the convention that it was traditional for the leader's wife to address the crowd, Olive was nonplussed. Despite all the lectures she had given in the past, she did not enjoy public speaking, and she was even less enthusiastic about being told what to do. "I decided I had to do it," she later said, "but that was it. After that I made up my own mind."

Early in 1957 party officials began to make plans for John and Olive's move into Stornoway, the official residence of the leader of the Opposition. When Olive heard the news she dug in her heels. Confident that John would soon be swept to power, she considered it foolish to move twice within so short a time. As it turned out, her instincts were right once again.

Politically she and John held largely the same views; and although Olive rarely discussed politics in public, she began to breathe much of her own force into John's policies. The brash manner that had surfaced from time to time during her years with the Department of Education disappeared from public view. In its place emerged a facade of discretion and diplomacy.

On the campaign trail she shared John's platform and passed notes to him reminding him of names and facts he had forgotten. Once, in Quebec, she stirred an audience to warm applause by speaking in acceptable French after John's effort to speak a few French words had met with frigid silence.

Her enthusiasm for meeting people made her a hit across the country. Often when she received a bouquet of flowers she would pass it on to an employee at the next hotel. As one reporter put it: "She never lost an opportunity to win a convert." Yet despite her efforts, Olive did not campaign as a political personality in her own right. "My job," she once told a friend, "is not a political one."

During a break in campaigning, she explained how she

stood the strain. "If you roll with the ship, it's good fun. People tell me it must be awful, hearing the same speech night after night. It isn't. Actually, it's fun seeing what variations John will make on the prepared text."

Although not all aspects of public life were as easily borne, the badinage she enjoyed with John helped her through some tense moments. Once at a luncheon in the Maritimes, she ate lobster with seeming enjoyment, despite the fact she was allergic to it. Half way through the meal John leaned over and noted her headway. "Have some more, dear," he urged. "No, thanks," she replied with arch cordiality. "Are you sure?" he jabbed. "There's lots more!"

As the election campaign of 1957 progressed, Olive redoubled her efforts on John's behalf, making scores of public appearances and writing thank you notes to anyone who had contributed even in a small way to the Conservative cause. Each time their train pulled into a station, Olive would be off in one direction, John in another. According to George Nowlan, Revenue Minister in the Diefenbaker Cabinet, she was "probably the best campaigner we had next to John."

When the polls finally closed on election night it became obvious the long weeks of work had paid off. After twenty-two years in Opposition, the Conservatives would finally form a government.

For Olive her official social duties were secondary to those of counsellor to the prime minister. Even so, she launched a vigorous entertainment program that saw eight hundred guests visit 24 Sussex Drive in the first three months of the Diefenbaker administration. Although she valued her privacy, she felt it was her "duty to show the house to those who can and should be here."

Her kindness and grace won the admiration of both reporters intent on a good story and diplomats eager for a good party. So successful was she as a hostess that at a dinner in honour of Queen Elizabeth and Prince Philip, the royal couple stayed behind, chatting amiably an hour after their scheduled departure.

According to one friend, Olive always took the time to help wives of new M.P.s adjust to Ottawa. Her ability to give advice tactfully and her sensitivity to the moods of others made her immensely popular.

In London just before she moved to Sussex Drive, she was assigned a car and a female driver. Squeezing through rush hour traffic, the chauffeur scraped the car and became visibly upset. At the end of the ride Olive unpinned an expensive brooch and with an understanding smile slipped it into the driver's hand.

The fact she attended a full round of public functions in London was amazing in itself. During the flight from Ottawa the plane had dropped five hundred feet, banging Olive's head against the ceiling. Two vertebrae were crushed and she was in severe pain for weeks.

As the years passed, John became dependent upon Olive for everything. Even on a short trip he wanted her with him for support and encouragement. To keep other demands to a minimum, Olive booked her social engagements for the afternoon, keeping the evenings free. "Things crop up suddenly in politics," she once said, "and my first responsibility is to do what John wants."

In her role as confidante, advisor, chatelaine and friend, she bore his dependence stoically. Often she would sit in bed reading or knitting while he worked far into the night. When he had put the last paper back in his briefcase, they would go into the tiny kitchenette adjoining their sitting room and set out a snack of cheese, crackers and milk.

One of the most distinguishing features of their relationship was the banter they traded. One exchange so delighted John that he related it to friends. "Olive was sitting at the foot of the table reciting a short prayer in her softest voice. 'I didn't hear you,' I needled. 'I wasn't talking to you,' she replied."

As John's term of office dragged on, Olive attended an ever growing number of luncheons, bazaars, jubilees and meetings. In recognition of her efforts one columnist dubbed her "the hardest working prime minister's wife in Canadian history." Another noted that "the prime minister's greatest achievement was in persuading her to become Mrs. Diefenbaker."

Yet as a wife, Olive was not without fault. From the earliest days of her marriage she resented anyone who criticized John, and opponents of the Conservative government automatically became her enemies. To make matter worse, she constantly reminded John of those who had slighted him, thus nurturing his antipathy of political critics.

There were other problems in their marriage as well. Constant political demands gnawed away at their time together, but more serious was the problem posed by John's mother. A stern, possessive woman, Mary Diefenbaker had made the life of John's first wife, Edna, a misery; she tried valiantly to have the same effect on Olive. During a stay in hospital, Mary called Olive to her bedside. With a picture of Edna on the night table, she praised the daughter-in-law she had so often slighted. "You could never be a patch on her!" she concluded.

When the Conservative government fell in 1963, Olive relinquished her official social duties. Four years later she bore John's defeat as leader of the Conservative Party with equal dignity and comforted supporters who could not mask their disappointment.

By 1975 her health had begun to deteriorate. With customary self-possession she prepared John for her death. Her greatest fear was that he would be left with no one to look after him. For the last eighteen months of her life she commuted between hospital and home. Yet despite the discomfort caused by a variety of ailments, she continued to attend the political functions that John considered necessary. On one occasion she left hospital prematurely to accompany him on a western tour. Far from discouraging her, John stressed his need for her company and praised her courage. On his eightieth birthday, he tried to express his gratitude for all she had sacrificed. "She's just an amazing woman. No one will ever know what she has done."

By the fall of 1976, however, the strain had become too much, and in October Olive was rushed to hospital with a serious heart condition. On December 20 she was released to spend Christmas at home. Two days later John began to call her from his office every fifteen minutes. During one conversation Olive asked to speak to Robert Coates, a prominent Conservative who had dropped in for a visit. "John keeps phoning me," she told him. "Can you do something to stop him? I'm really not up to it."

She put down the receiver and joined her housekeeper and nurse in the kitchen for lunch. The three women were laughing and enjoying the meal when Olive suddenly felt faint. The spoon fell from her hand and within seconds she was dead.

Funeral services were held at First Baptist Church in Ottawa on Christmas Eve, and she was buried later that day in Beechwood Cemetery near their home in Ottawa. For two and a half years her body lay undisturbed.

Then, on August 16, 1979, John died at the age of eighty-three. In accordance with his wishes, he was buried on a grassy knoll overlooking the Saskatchewan River. As the mourners approached the graveside they gazed quizzically at a second coffin draped in black crepe. The body of Olive Diefenbaker had been exhumed and at John's request was being reinterred with his.

MARYON PEARSON

On March 31, 1958, Mike and Maryon Pearson sat in a private suite at the Chateau Laurier in downtown Ottawa eating oyster stew and watching the election returns on television. As the polls closed across the country and one Liberal stronghold after another fell to the Conservatives, Maryon's hopes secretly soared. With a little luck maybe Mike would lose his seat in Algoma East and that, coupled with what was shaping up as a defeat for the Liberal Party, might be enough to get him to leave politics for good.

When word was finally received hours later that Mike had retained his seat but that the Conservatives had won the election, Maryon turned to him with a shrug. "We've lost everything," she said bitterly. "We've even won our own seat."

Maryon Pearson was in many respects the most reluctant prime minister's wife in Canadian history. Valuing her privacy above all else, she resented the intrusion politics made into her personal life. Although she respected Mike's love of the political process and usually presented her best face at Liberal gatherings, she was occasionally unable to prevent her true feelings from showing through. Once, after a hectic day of rallies and meetings she was asked if she would like to bring anything up before she left. "Yes," she replied wryly, "the last five cups of coffee."

Maryon Elspeth Moody was born in Winnipeg, Manitoba, in 1901. The second of three children, she grew up in a comfortable upper middle-class home and entertained vague dreams of one day becoming a writer.

Maryon Pearson

Her father, A.W. Moody, was an ambitious, hardworking Englishman who immigrated to Canada in the 1880s and put himself through medical school. He eventually became superintendent of the Winnipeg General Hospital and married the superintendent of nurses who was also English by birth.

Maryon was always her father's favourite. She was petite and mischievous and at an early age began to show shades of a vibrant, outspoken personality. Shortly before her eighteenth birthday she enrolled, at her father's urging, at Victoria College, University of Toronto. Working toward her arts degree, she decided in her fourth year to take a history course conducted by Lester B. Pearson, a young professor who also coached the football and hockey teams.

Pearson was immediately attracted to the animated, self-possessed young woman with the wistful, often cynical smile and the large, observant eyes; and in March, 1924, the two announced their engagement.

They both wanted to set an early date for the wedding, but Maryon's mother, a staunch Victorian, believed that Maryon's older sister, Grace, who was also engaged, should be the first to marry. Mike (a nickname Pearson acquired during World War I) and Maryon were given their choice — wait until after Grace was married or take part in a double ceremony. Unwilling to delay things any longer than necessary, they chose the latter and on August 22, 1925 were married in Winnipeg.

After a brief honeymoon, the newlyweds moved into a flat on the top floor of an old Victorian house, and Mike resumed his position at the University of Toronto. From the beginning Maryon took over management of the household. She controlled the purse strings, superintended their social life, picked out Mike's suits, and in later years picked out the family car.

In the summer of 1926 she and Mike went to Ottawa to research a book he wanted to write on the United Empire Loyalists. During their stay Mike slipped away several times to the House of Commons and in the visitors' gallery experienced the excitement of political and parliamentary life. Although he began to follow the policies of the government with great attention, he gave no thought to actually entering politics himself, and at the end of the summer he and Maryon returned to Toronto where they picked up the threads of what they believed would remain their quiet life in academia.

The following spring Maryon found out that she was pregnant. For months she read everything she could find on child care and parenting, and when she finally went into labour on December 24, 1927, she and Mike were ecstatic — they would have a Christmas baby.

After the birth of her first son, Maryon emerged from the anesthetic only to discover that she was still in the delivery room. Groggily she raised herself on an elbow and looked around. There, in a corner huddled together discussing the prospects of the university hockey team were Mike and the doctor. With a few well chosen words she let them know that she was awake and in need of attention, and for years after Mike's gaffe remained the butt of family jokes.

A few weeks after she and the baby returned home, Maryon found out that Mike was considering writing examinations being held in Ottawa in June to fill the positions of first and third secretaries in the Department of External Affairs. At the time, the whole matter seemed unimportant to her. Then, when word came in August that he had been appointed first secretary, she faced a difficult decision. She knew that Mike, who had recently been promoted to assistant professor and director of athletics at almost double his original salary, would be guided by her opinion. If they stayed where they were, she was afraid that his position as director of athletics would gradually supersede his teaching — an eventuality she found extremely distasteful. If he took the new job, it would mean leaving their quiet academic life forever. In the end, she agreed that he should join the civil service.

Once settled in Ottawa, she found life more hectic than it had been in Toronto. The cadre of Mike's job required them to lead a more active social life than either of them enjoyed, and Maryon especially faced a difficult adjustment. She had always preferred the companionship of a few close friends to moving in large social circles, and she dreaded what lay ahead. Beneath her candour and self-possession lay her essential shyness and introversion, and her refusal to adapt to the frivolous, insincere social life of the capital led to criticism that she was tempermental and standoffish. Only those who were really close to her understood that while she was vivacious and witty with those she knew, she was uncomfortable in larger groups and consequently appeared formal and reserved. As one friend put it, "Maryon is completely incapable of acting." Another, describing life in the diplomatic corps said, "In our little world of polished brass, Maryon Pearson is a genuine nugget."

For a time, however, Maryon was able to keep her social activities to a minimum. She was pregnant with her second child and for several months was able to retire to private life. When she finally returned to the social whirl in 1930, she found the pace more hectic than she remembered. The demands of Mike's job had grown dramatically, leaving him little time to devote to domestic life, and more and more of the social burden was thrust upon Maryon.

Finally, in 1935, Mike was transferred to London. Maryon quickly adapted to life in England, and although she was critical of the class consciousness she found, she was relieved to find the pressures of diplomatic life less onerous than they had been in Ottawa. The great size of London seemed to swallow up the diplomatic circle and to give her more time to herself. As she later told a reporter, "London gives you a life of your own."

In 1939 she and Mike decided to take the children back to Canada for a summer holiday. Soon after their arrival, however, Nazi threats against Danzig and the Polish corridor sent Mike rushing back to London. Several months later, after war had been officially declared, Maryon left the children with relatives in Winnipeg and joined him in London.

By June, 1940, the situation in England had begun to deteriorate, and Mike felt the time had come for her to return to Winnipeg. Maryon greeted the suggestion with undisguised fury. She felt that her place was with him and she saw no reason why she should be sent home. After some very heated discussions, Mike finally convinced her that her first duty was to the children, and late in the summer she sailed for Canada.

Although their separation did not end until Mike was recalled to Ottawa a year later, the first moments of their reunion were tentative and strained. Embarrassed by deep emotion, Maryon often tried to hide her true feelings. When she saw Mike, she took one look at him and told him he needed a haircut.

They bought a new home and had just readjusted to life in Ottawa when Mike was transferred to Washington to serve first as Minister-Counsellor and finally as Ambassador. To prevent themselves from being caught in the same social bind they had been in Ottawa, they abbreviated their activities to suit their own taste. As hosts, they substituted small luncheons and receptions for formal parties, and as guests they spent as little time away from home as they could. Yet, for all this, the Pearsons were not recluses. They enjoyed being at the centre of important political events; the problem lay in the fact they were never able to think of Washington as home.

Another aspect of diplomatic life that Marion did not enjoy was submitting to interviews. Asked by a reporter for the *Washington Post* in 1942 to give her impression of the American capital, she replied: "Well, it must have been a lovely city before the war. It really would be a pleasant city if it were not so crowded." Some members of the press, affronted by her remarks, denounced her reply as tart and catty, and her cool relationship with the press was officially established.

Despite the demands Mike's position forced upon her, Maryon was still very protective of his career. Once, at a United Nations Relief and Rehabilitation Administrative Council meeting she attended with him, she sat in silence as he agreed to preside over the discussions — but on the condition that no one raise a point of order. Explaining that he felt they were a waste of time and that he knew virtually nothing about rules of order and procedure, he went on to open the first session. A little while later Maryon disappeared from the meeting. When she returned she discreetly beckoned to a messenger and asked him to slip a parcel to Mike. Inside was a comprehensive booklet entitled, "Parliamentary Procedure at a Glance."

A few months after the meeting, Mike was recalled to Canada and in 1946, at the age of forty-nine, was named Under Secretary of State for External Affairs. Once back in Ottawa, Maryon decided to do her part to make life in the diplomatic corps more agreeable and egalitarian. To compensate for the snobbery that prevented second secretaries and other lesser lights from attending formal diplomatic functions, she formed the Ottawa Dance Club and participated with unwonted enthusiasm in the group's frequent gatherings.

Then in 1948 Mike's career threatened to intrude even further into their private life: Mackenzie King had offered him a Cabinet post. For long days and nights he and Maryon wrestled with the pros and cons of the situation. A friend once described Maryon as a woman who considered every problem from the standpoint of Mike's welfare, and with this latest decision facing her she responded in characteristic style. Although she would have preferred him to stay in the civil service, she knew his heart was set on the Cabinet appointment and in the end she agreed that he should take it.

On September 10, 1948, Mike was sworn in as Secretary of State for External Affairs, and a byelection was called to make way for him in the House of Commons. In the campaign that followed Maryon worked diligently to ensure his victory, but the job was not easy. Crowds frightened her and she found shaking hands with strangers and smiling during endless rallies both taxing and boring. She was often stiff and shy, and she made no secret of her distaste for politics. Once during her campaigning she remarked bitterly: "What a terrible waste of Mike all this is." She did not see why it was necessary for a politician's wife to take an active part in campaigning, but because Mike and the electorate expected it, she made the effort. Her only compensation was being at the centre of activity. "If you stay at home," she once said, "you never know what's really happening."

Maryon did more, however, than appear with her husband at political rallies. At Mike's request she reviewed his speeches before they were delivered, and, according to Mike, wrote in all the jokes.

When the election was finally over Maryon wondered about the wisdom of their decision to leave the civil service. The demands of his new job forced Mike to work frequently during the evening and he often brought home files full of documents.

To make matters worse, the social responsibilities associated with his new position were more tedious than those associated with his job in Washington, and Maryon soon became more protective than ever of their private life. While many politicians' wives created masks to wear on different occasions, Maryon refused to compromise herself. At every juncture she presented her true face.

Her insecurity in large groups did not lessen with time and she remained a reluctant socialite. Once, en route with then Health and Welfare Minister Paul Martin to a luncheon for U.N. Secretary General Trygvie Lie, she began to tremble. When Martin leaned over and asked what was wrong she replied: "I'm always like this. I never know how I'm going to face up to all those people until I get there."

In 1953 she found herself facing larger crowds than ever before. It was election year and despite the fact she continued to dislike campaigning, she was determined to again accompany Mike to the hustings. At many of the meetings she appeared stiff and reserved, but although she found it difficult to strike up conversation with strangers, the constituents recognized her shyness and responded to her warmly.

When the polls finally closed on election night, she sat in front of the television with Mike and anxiously awaited the results. As the hours dragged by she turned her attention to one area in the riding where they had received an especially warm welcome. The results from that particular polling station — one hundred and ten votes for Mike as compared with four for his opponent — satisfied everyone by Maryon. Always a perfectionist, she furrowed her brow. "I wonder who those four could have been," she murmured.

With the Liberal victory at the polls, she continued to perform the social duties of a Cabinet minister's wife, and until the government was defeated in 1957 travelled extensively with Mike on official business. When the day finally came on June 17, 1957 for St. Laurent (who had succeeded King as prime minister) and his ministers to make the slow march to Rideau Hall to present their resignations to the governor general, Mike's career as a cabinet minister came officially to an end. Later that day, Maryon, tongue in cheek, called him at his office and suggested that as he now had more time for domestic life, he stop at a supermarket on the way home and pick up some hamburger.

In 1958 Mike was chosen to replace Louis St. Laurent as leader of the Liberal Party, and he and Maryon moved into

Stornoway, the official residence of the leader of the Opposition. From the first time she saw the house, Maryon developed a deep affection for it. A year and a half of neglect following the departure of the previous tenants had left it in poor repair, but Maryon recognized the potential and immediately set about restoring and redecorating.

They had their own furniture installed and once the art collection they had been gathering over the years was in place, they both felt at home. The demands on her time were less than they had been for several years and Maryon took up painting. Although she felt she had no real talent, she enjoyed the luxury of finally being able to indulge herself.

It was during her time at Stornoway that she came to the conclusion it was important for Mike to realize his ambition of becoming prime minister. She still preferred life in the diplomatic service to life in the public eye, and would have chosen life in academia above all else, but Mike — as always — was her first consideration and if he wanted to become prime minister, she would not stand in his way.

When the Diefenbaker government finally went down to defeat in February, 1963, Mike and Maryon realized that Mike's chances of becoming prime minister were as good as they were ever going to be. They campaigned vigorously and by the time the general election was held on April 8 were both exhausted.

As the first results trickled in from Newfoundland, the Liberals seemed to be in a good position. Maryon fixed Mike a poached egg, then sent him off with his press officer to Liberal Headquarters. While returns continued to come in from the Atlantic Provinces, she prepared a light meal for herself, then changed her clothes and joined Mike and his aides in a back room to watch the rest of the results on television.

When the political commentator announced over the full CBC network that he could not understand what had caused the Social Credit Party to make such a poor showing in Montreal, Maryon leaned forward in her chair and boomed: "Common sense caused it!"

Later, she and Mike moved into a suite at the Chateau Laurier and braced themselves as the Conservatives began to pick up support. As the night dragged on Norman DePoe appeared on television and told a nationwide audience: "The west seems to be sticking to Mr. Diefenbaker." Maryon glanced over at Mike and crinkled her nose. "The dirty dogs!" she spluttered.

From that point on, the situation improved for the Liberals and it soon became clear that Mike and Maryon would be the new residents of 24 Sussex Drive.

Shortly before they moved into the prime minister's official residence, Maryon took a private tour of the house. Drawing up a list of the improvements she wanted made, she quickly realized that she had a major job ahead of her. She found the decor too cold and formal and felt the whole place was too officially elegant. With characteristic gusto she rearranged and reupholstered the furniture and created a new atmosphere of warmth and grace.

Her greatest triumph was in the official drawing and dining rooms where she stripped the walls of their cold gilt mirrors and replaced them with colorful Canadian paintings borrowed from the National Gallery. She later acquired another painting for the house when officials of the City of Toronto decided to present the new prime minister and his wife with a gift. Fearing she would have to find room for a silver tea service or something equally redundant, Maryon asked if they could have what they really wanted — another Canadian painting.

Although she did not pretend to be a connoisseur, Maryon *did* acknowledge her interest in art. She once told a university professor that as the prime minister's wife she would like to turn Sussex Drive into a centre for the arts just as Jacqueline Kennedy had done in the White House. A lack of public funding, however, prevented her from ever making the dream a reality. An ambition she *was* able to realize was the construction of a Canadiana room at Sussex Drive. Designed to encourage handicrafts and to give recognition to artisans of the past, the room is filled with early French Canadian furniture and was created as her own centennial project.

Largely, however, she viewed her new life with distaste. She missed her own furniture, which had been put in storage, and pined for the freedom to be able to putter about the house at will. She once confided that she felt housework was good for

135

a person physically and that with a staff of six to take care of all the domestic duties she resented not being able to do anything for herself. She described life at Sussex Drive as similar to life in a hotel and admitted that apart from the view the house afforded she would be glad to leave when Mike's term expired.

Privacy was nonexistent and she found the social demands of her position took up even more time than she had anticipated. She disliked the intrusion made on her private life and was especially annoyed when weekly bridge games with old friends had to be dropped to allow more time for attending official luncheons and dinners.

It was only in the family's private sitting room and at the prime minister's official summer residence at Harrington Lake that she felt free to be herself. There and only there could she cast aside formality and completely relax. Dressed in slacks, she would read and watch television and occasionally tackle cryptic crosswords.

On the political front the most aggravating moments in her life came when she sat in the gallery of the House of Commons and listened to the proceedings. The needless waste of time and the meaningless arguments frustrated her and she could only take the sessions in small doses. Attacks on the government in general and on Mike in particular triggered her notoriously short temper and she made it clear to the press that she considered the attacks all "terribly unfair."

Rarely during public appearances did her self-possession fail her. Once, however, during a rally in Vancouver an antagonistic crowd heckled Mike and attacked him with pea-shooters. The scene became ugly and Maryon was reduced to tears. For weeks afterward the experience burned in her memory and her protectiveness of Mike was strengthened even further.

She closely followed what was printed in the newspapers about him and once admitted that the criticism upset her much more than it did him. The political cartoons especially annoyed her — she could never understand why they portrayed Mike as such a "frightfully dishevelled old creature." During a visit to London she vented her spleen on the press for being "always at the prime minister" and added: "Sometimes I think how marvelous it would be to get all the newspaper editors together and form a Cabinet and see how *they* could run the country."

The bluntness of her statements earned her a great deal of negative publicity — especially in light of the fact that her most recent predecessors, Mrs. St. Laurent and Mrs. Diefenbaker, had been more circumspect in their comments. One person who was not appalled by her candour was Charles Ritchie, the Canadian diplomat, who once described her as "very funny and very much on the mark in her comments."

Undeterred by the controversy she created, Maryon continued to do and say as she pleased. Her interest in Mike, his job, and the problems that went with it prompted her to voice her opinion to him on a wide variety of topics. When the flag debate was at its height, she told him that she preferred a flag with blue bars on either end because she liked the sea to sea symbolism.

Mike ignored her advice and Maryon took his decision with good grace. What he did politically was his business, not hers. Her chief concern was protecting and supporting him. When she thought he had made a good speech she told him so; when she thought he had made a bad one, she said nothing. She felt he received enough negative criticism without getting more from her.

As the years passed the subject of Mike's retirement was much on Maryon's mind. Together they decided he would step down when he turned seventy and she looked forward to their return to private life. In 1968 Mike announced that he was finally leaving and after a leadership convention officially handed over the reins of power to Pierre Trudeau.

A few days later he and Maryon left on a long overdue vacation. Cherishing the uninterrupted days together, they realized how right the decision to retire had been. For a time after their return to Ottawa Mike missed the excitement of being in the centre of the political scene, but he soon directed his energies to writing his memoirs and worked on them steadily until his death in 1972.

In February, 1973, for the first time in several years, Maryon sat in the visitors' gallery of the House of Commons to take part in a ceremony commemorating the eighth anniversary of the official raising of the Canadian flag. Later that year she again appeared in public to present Mike's private papers to the National Archives and afterward returned to the security of life away from the public eye.

MARGARET TRUDEAU

Margaret Trudeau was the most controversial prime minister's wife in Canadian history. Her unorthodox behavior and off the cuff comments made headlines around the world and earned her the nickname "Princess Flower Child." While some observers hailed her as a free spirit, many others denounced her as a spoiled brat. The real Margaret Trudeau lies somewhere in between.

The daughter of James and Doris Sinclair, Margaret was born in Vancouver on September 10, 1948. Although her father was a Liberal Member of Parliament (and later a Cabinet minister), politics were rarely discussed at home. Mrs. Sinclair maintained that government policy should be debated in the Commons, not in her living room.

While Margaret was growing up, her parents were comfortable — not affluent — and one of her earliest memories is of being forced to wear clothes handed down from her three older sisters. Another thing that stands out in her mind is the lack of attention she received from her parents. Her position as the fourth of five children led to her being frequently forgotten; and as she grew older, the perceived neglect made her extremely sensitive.

Not surprisingly, the exuberance of a large family was often too much for her; and she found the noise of seven people talking at the dinner table unbearable. Rock music was easier on her nerves: like most fourteen-year-old girls in 1962, she idolized the Beatles.

Hand-me-down clothes eventually became a source of contention with her; and to ensure that she did not wear culls,

Margaret Trudeau

she began making dresses of her own. Nothing but the finest materials satisfied her. She later said that she believed her teenage preoccupation with her appearance was an effort to cover up her feelings of confusion, rivalry and inadequacy.

As a student, Margaret did well. She skipped grade three and is remembered by her teachers as a conscientious pupil and one who was popular with her classmates. When she was in grade ten, she began attending chaperoned parties and flirting with boys. Perhaps because she had grown up without brothers, she found it impossible to look upon boys as friends; and, as a result, dating did not particularly appeal to her.

In 1965, Margaret graduated from high school and enrolled at Simon Fraser University. She won a scholarship during her first year and excelled in sociology. Then, in 1966, she was carried along in the wake of a wave of student activism that hit the campus. Although she did not participate in the sit-ins, she rebelled at home by questioning life and politics in a way that infuriated her father. Eventually, she moved out on her own and began experimenting with marijuana and mescaline.

The following year, she went with her parents to Tahiti on a trip designed to heal the rift that had developed between them. One afternoon, as she lay sunbathing, a man came up to her and started talking about student rebellion and revolution. Mrs. Sinclair, watching from a distance, recognized the man as Pierre Elliott Trudeau, the Canadian justice minister. When she later told her daughter, Margaret was unimpressed. In her eyes, Pierre, then forty-seven, was "old" and "square." She stood him up when he invited her deep-sea fishing and did not see him again until the Liberal leadership convention was held in April. As Margaret tells it, she was waiting in a hallway for her parents when he passed by, surrounded by delegates. Suddenly he noticed her, swept through the crowd, kissed her on both cheeks, and hurried on. Within hours, he had become both leader of the Liberal Party and prime minister of Canada. Margaret was pleased by his attention but not bowled over.

In December, 1968, she left for hippie-infested Morocco. If she was looking for paradise, she was soon disillusioned. The filth appalled her, and she found herself making a fetish of personal hygiene. Drifting from place to place, living on next to nothing, smoking keef and taking LSD, she believed she was enjoying total freedom. After seven months, however, the emptiness and promiscuity of her hippie existence began to pall on her; and she finally returned to Vancouver. Predictably, her parents frowned upon her adventures. A second falling out developed and Margaret went to live with her maternal grandmother on the Sechelt Peninsula. Then, one day, her mother called to say that Pierre Trudeau wanted Margaret to go out to dinner with him. Margaret considered for a few moments before deciding to accept the invitation. She went shopping with her mother and had her hair done; but when she was finally ready, she looked in the mirror and gagged. In her opinion, she looked like a Barbie doll.

Fortunately, Pierre did not remind her of a Ken doll. Oozing confidence with his first year as prime minister behind him, he no longer struck Margaret as "old" and "square." The awkwardness she felt when he arrived to pick her up disappeared as they entered the restaurant and began talking of student revolution and Morocco. Margaret believed she had found a friend. Yet despite Pierre's affability, she discovered herself totally in awe of him. She was later to admit that she felt the same awe the entire six years they lived together. By the end of the evening, she knew she wanted to see more of the prime minister; and within weeks, she had moved to Ottawa and gone to work for the Department of Manpower and Immigration as a sociologist.

One day, she called Pierre. He invited her to 24 Sussex Drive for a spaghetti dinner and a grand tour of the house. By Christmas they were in love but doubtful of the future. Then, early in 1970, their relationship cooled; and Margaret halfheartedly announced her engagement to a divinity student. She reconciled with Pierre during the Easter holidays; and in the summer, they began talking of marriage. According to Margaret, Pierre made it clear she would have to stop using drugs and cautioned her that life as wife of the prime minister would be difficult.

To make sure that marriage was what they both wanted, they decided to keep their feelings secret and to have a quiet wedding when they felt ready. Finally, on March 4, 1971, they were married in a private ceremony at St. Stephen's Roman Catholic Church in Vancouver. Margaret's mother warned her that she was making a mistake, and Pierre told her that she would eventually leave him. But Margaret was young and in love, and she ignored them both.

After a three-day honeymoon, she and Pierre flew back to Ottawa. At the time, all Margaret wanted was to turn what she called Pierre's cold, lonely life into a warm, happy one. Suddenly, however, she found herself face to face with the reality of her situation. The youngest prime minister's wife in Canadian history and, in 1971, the youngest wife of a head of state in the Western world, she had to familiarize herself not only with protocol, but also with the secrets of running a large household. Within weeks, she realized that she was in over her head. Every other Canadian prime minister's wife had had at least *some* time to prepare for her husband's rise to power. Margaret had been dragged into the melee after only the briefest of honeymoons. Life as the daughter of a Member of Parliament had done nothing to prepare her for marriage to the prime minister. She became nervous and unpredictable and experienced feelings of inadequacy. In later years, she felt tense even when she was playing alone with her children.

To make matters worse, she was an object of curiosity. Pierre tried to protect her privacy by clamping an embargo on her. Unlike previous prime ministers' wives, her social schedule was severely restricted. No one was allowed to bother her: no one was allowed to go near her. Margaret, then shy and retiring, was probably relieved to be able to stay out of the spotlight. Yet with few personal friends in Ottawa, she was often lonely.

The only person who tried to make life easier for her was Norah Michener, wife of the governor general, Roland Michener. In one tête-à-tête after another, Mrs. Michener initiated Margaret to the mysteries of protocol. Margaret took the lessons to heart and vowed to become not only the perfect prime minister's wife, but also the most perfect wife in the world. Allowing herself no margin for error, she was bound to fall short.

With each passing week, her loneliness grew, and she realized a little bit more just how unenviable the life of the prime minister's wife really was. Then, one day, Pierre told her that if she were ever kidnapped and held for ransom he would make no deals, offer no amnesty. Stunned by the vulnerability of her situation, Margaret asked if he would actually let her die rather than agree to terms. Pierre replied that he would. The October crisis of 1970 was still foremost on his mind, and he felt it was morally wrong to buckle under to terrorists. Margaret understood his reasons, but his words did not add to her peace of mind.

When her first child, Justin, was born on Christmas Day, 1971, Margaret became front-page news. The announcement that she was breast-feeding the baby met with even better reviews, and she was quickly held up as a model of Canadian motherhood. As time passed, however, she became something of a laughingstock when it was revealed that she was nursing Justin ten or more times a day and that she frequently excused herself from the dinner table to go to him. When her second son, Sacha, was born on Christmas Day, 1973, she was again restored to public favor.

Yet despite the attention she received when her children were born, Margaret did not see an end to her purdah-like seclusion. Had she hopped on a streetcar, the average Canadian would not have recognized her. Just how low a profile she had been forced to keep became obvious during the 1972 election campaign when she arrived at a Vancouver hotel to join Pierre, who had checked in earlier. First the elevator operator and then the desk clerk refused to direct her to the prime minister's suite. Finally, Margaret asked for the assistant manager. When he, too, failed to recognize her, she announced who she was and asked to be taken to her husband. Amidst a flurry of apologies, she was escorted to the correct suite.

Clearly the time had come for her to emerge from the cocoon Pierre had so carefully spun around her. During the last days of the campaign, she unexpectedly jumped out of her chauffeur-driven limousine, climbed aboard the press bus that was following the official motorcade and held an impromptu press conference. She told reporters that she wanted to set the record straight — she ws not a milquetoast. Instead, she considered herself rather fiery. "I'm not public property," she went on, "and I'm not my husband's property either." She had finally given vent to a growing urge to explain her thoughts and feelings.

A month later, she admitted to herself that, although she had a husband who loved her and a wonderful baby, she was unhappy and still very lonely. As it turned out, things would only get worse.

She did eke out some happiness, however, in 1973 when she accompanied Pierre on a trip to China. Seven and a half months pregnant with her second child, she toured a maternity hospital in Peking. Through her interpreter, she asked a doctor what they did with cases of RH incompatibility. (She had experienced a blood problem with Justin.) When the doctor replied that they did nothing — the babies died — Margaret was flabbergasted. In precise detail, she explained how the RH Disease Centre in Winnipeg had discovered a way to prevent death by inoculating within two hours of birth. The doctor's interest was immediately aroused; and later that day, Margaret arranged for the Canadian deputy minister of health to have vaccine and information sent to Peking.

By the time the election campaign began in 1974, Margaret was showing the first signs of what she later called her "rebellion." When she was asked to speak in public, she would say the first thing that came into her mind. Often her comments were too frank; and when they were, the press pounced on her.

In Humboldt, Saskatchewan, where Pierre delivered a tedious speech prepared by the minister in charge of the Wheat Board, Margaret sat on the platform waiting for her turn at the microphone. "I must apologize," she said sarcastically when her opportunity finally came, "but neither the good minister here nor his lovely wife have been kind enough to write an elegant speech for me to make." While the official party stiffened and reporters scribbled, the crowd roared its approval.

The Liberal victory at the polls caused Margaret mixed feelings. Although she wanted to live a normal life away from the public eye, she realized the importance to the country of Pierre's return to power. In the aftermath of the election, she felt used, her emotions were in a turmoil; and in September, the

145

prime minister's office announced that she had checked into hospital for "rest and some tests." When members of the media began to suspect that something more serious was wrong, Margaret again made headlines by revealing that she was suffering from severe depression and was staying in the psychiatric unit. Twelve days later, she was back at 24 Sussex Drive determined, as she told reporters, not to allow herself to be used anymore.

In October, she agreed to appear on CTV's public affairs program, "W-5". During the interview she spoke candidly, often indiscreetly, about her breakdown, life at 24 Sussex Drive, her Moroccan trip, and what it was like being a flower child. She was fully aware of the shock value of her comments; and in the months that followed, her words and antics outraged Canadians. In an interview with *People* magazine, she revealed that wearing a garter belt and stockings turned her on; while during an official visit to Latin America, she snapped to attention and gave an exaggerated salute when the Canadian national anthem was playing at the start of a state dinner.

Finally, on a trip to Venezuela in 1976 — three months after her son, Michel was born — she sang a song praising Mrs. Perez, wife of President Carlos Perez, for her social consciousness. Although Mrs. Perez was charmed, Canadians were scandalized; and when Margaret returned to Ottawa, she listened in fury as a caller to an open-line radio show condemned her behavior. When the host invited Margaret to rebut the criticism, she seized the telephone, dialed the number and launched into a bitter tirade. Suddenly a new controversy had arisen over the propriety of the prime minister's wife participating in talk shows. Margaret was fed up. No matter what she did or said, she was wrong. She had one consolation: as the criticism grew stronger, her tongue grew sharper.

Inevitably, her rebellion began to affect her marriage. She and Pierre argued and their feelings toward one another became bitter. To try and ease the pressure, Margaret decided to find a new outlet for her energy. In January, 1977, she enrolled in a photography course at Algonquin College as a full-time student. It was now impossible for her to attend daytime functions held in Ottawa and all functons held outside.

146

It was a last-ditch effort to save her marriage by putting distance between herself and politics. In the end, it failed. On their sixth wedding anniversary — March 4, 1977 — she and Pierre agreed to a ninety-day trial separation. Margaret packed her clothes and headed for Toronto. After a much publicized weekend with the Rolling Stones, she went to New York and started attending drama classes.

The press followed her night and day as she went from one party to another. She was moving at a frenzied pace, desperately trying to outrun her resentment and insecurity. At the same time, she was looking for a new identity — trying to prove that Margaret Trudeau was an individual, not a rose on Pierre's label. On May 27, 1977, the prime minister's office announced that Margaret and Pierre had officially separated and that Margaret had relinquished "all privileges as wife of the prime minister." It was agreed that Pierre would have custody of the children.

After appearing to poor reviews in two disastrous movies, writing a two-volume autobiography, and giving a score of interviews, each more outrageous than the last, Margaret finally settled down. By the fall of 1981 her life had returned to a state of normalcy, and she declared that her "wild days" were behind her. Somehow, she had come to grips with herself. She told a reporter that although her previous behavior had been an attempt to find herself, she had gone overboard. Her greatest regret was that she had attracted so much publicity.

She bought a house in Ottawa and became co-host of a locally produced television show, "Morning Magazine." She saw more of the children and began to develop a closer relationship with them. In 1983 she was given her own early afternoon show, "Margaret." Her confidence returned and with it, her happiness.

When Pierre announced his decision to resign as prime minister early in 1984, Margaret told an interviewer that she was pleased for her sons because they would finally be able to enjoy a normal life. A month later, she and Pierre were quietly divorced; and on April 18, she married Fried Kemper, a successful Ottawa property developer. Describing her new husband as the best thing that ever happened to her, Margaret

147

also revealed that the anger and bitterness she and Pierre used to feel toward one another had disappeared.

The birth of her fourth son, Kyle Kemper, marked the beginning of a new family life for Margaret. She sees her sons by Pierre at least every other weekend; and when she is not busy with the children, she spends her time cooking, reading, and visiting friends. A housekeeper frees her of domestic drudgery.

Today, Margaret Kemper bears little resemblance to either Margaret Sinclair or Margaret Trudeau. While she has retained the spontaneity of her Vancouver days and remembers the lessons learned during the years at 24 Sussex Drive, she has emerged from the shadow of the past and has accomplished what she has always wanted — to stand as a person in her own right.

MAUREEN McTEER

During the nine months she lived at 24 Sussex Drive, Maureen McTeer shocked as many Canadians as Margaret Trudeau had in six years. Although she did not sing at state dinners or associate with rock stars of questionable character, she *did* have the audacity to keep her own surname and to voice her views on women's rights. Many people — especially males over the age of fifteen — saw her as a threat to the structure of Canadian society.

Born in Cumberland, Ontario in 1952, Maureen spent her childhood on the family farm, twenty miles east of Ottawa. Her parents, John and Bea McTeer, saw to it that their five daughters and one son earned their keep by performing chores and helping out around the house. At their father's insistence, all six children attended a one-room French school. Mr. McTeer felt it was essential that they become bilingual, and he believed that total immersion was the best way of achieving that goal.

Maureen, stubborn and determined even as a child, worked hard for the things she wanted. In 1963, she entered a hula-hoop contest. Plumper and more awkward than many of the other competitors, she thrust out her chin, wiggled her hips and by sheer force of will outlasted the others and took home the prize. When hula-hoops lost their appeal, she turned to debating. The local 4H club had its own team and Maureen soon became lead speaker. At the age of twelve, she began to share her father's interest in politics. They attended Progressive Conservative meetings together, argued about

Maureen McTeer

party principles and worked on John's two unsuccessful attempts to win election to the local council.

Personal freedom was important to Maureen; and when her parents imposed an 11 p.m. curfew in 1968, she went to Ottawa, moved in with her grandmother and attended an English high school. Two years later, she enrolled at the University of Ottawa. Her intense belief in her right to privacy kept her away from trendy group soul-searching, while her abrasiveness helped hold her classmates at bay. She knew exactly what she wanted in life and had no time for the student demonstrations popular at the time. Working on the campus paper and in the youth wing of the Ontario Progressive Conservative Party, she found outlets for her two main interests — writing and politics.

In 1972, while working toward her last degree credits, she went to work as a constituency assistant for an M.P. who had just arrived in Ottawa — Joe Clark. One evening they went out to dinner in Hull together and on the way back to Ottawa lost their way. It took an R.C.M.P. officer to put them back on the right road.

While Joe eventually found that his assistant could be caustic, he also discovered that she could be extremely cordial. He later said that she got along well with his constituents and worked tenaciously to solve their problems. The interest he and Maureen shared in politics drew them closer together; and they were married on June 30, 1973, a few weeks after Maureen graduated from the University of Ottawa with her Bachelor of Arts degree.

Impressed by his wife's self-assurance, Joe shared her belief in the need for sexual equality. Together, they made a strong political team. Maureen quickly made it clear, however, that although she would support Joe completely, she would do it as an individual, not as a hero-worshiper. She had her own goals and wanted to involve more Canadians — especially women — in the political process. She developed a deep interest in family law reform and in amendments to the sexual offences section of the Criminal Code. To prepare herself more fully for doing battle on feminist issues, she enrolled in law school at the University of Ottawa in the fall of 1973.

151

She was in the last year of her studies when Joe decided to run for the leadership of the Progressive Conservative Party. They both believed that with work and willpower he could win. Early in 1976 Maureen withdrew from university and went to work on Joe's campaign. Throwing herself headlong into the melee, she wasted no opportunity to win a convert. She expressed her own opinions and voiced her own concerns.

There was nothing new in wives campaigning for their husbands, but none had ever done it before as a political figure in her own right. Behind the scenes, aides resented Maureen's advice; and when they suggested she mind her own business, Maureen countered by suggesting they mind theirs. She appeared in as many places as she could. By speaking as an individual, not as a representative of her husband, she won widespread support and raised her own profile. When Joe finally won the leadership on the fourth ballot, it was as much Maureen's victory as it was his. He later said that without her, he would never have won.

After the convention, Maureen told a group of reporters that she and Joe had an equal relationship — one in which they reached all major decisions together. She anticipated personal questions by revealing that she and her husband did not enjoy dancing, sports events or the company of incompatible people. As time later proved, it was one of her rare discussions of her personal life. She valued her privacy and was not about to follow in Margaret Trudeau's footsteps by divulging intimate details of her life to the media. She did not attempt, however, to downplay her feminist principles; and when members of the party hierarchy asked her to change her surname to Clark, she firmly refused.

On the day she finally moved into Stornoway, the official residence of the leader of the Opposition, Maureen was twenty-four years old and pregnant with her first child. She soon found that in her new role the very force of her personality antagonized people, while the fierce protectiveness she evinced whenever her husband was attacked led to unkind comments. One of the few admirers of her possessive defensiveness of Joe was Margaret Trudeau, who wistfully reflected that perhaps such an attitude was one of the few solutions to a successful political marriage.

As a mother, Maureen appeared to be less tense. After her baby was born in 1976, she accepted the fact that the heavy demands of her time made a nanny essential. Yet with characteristic determination, she made sure that she was the one the baby grew to rely on. Birthday parties, special outings and frequent quiet times together were always worked into Maureen's schedule.

Not even motherhood, however, could lessen her interest in politics. Unfortunately, her interest often led to harsh criticism. When she was depicted by the press in 1979 as the Eva Peron of the North, Maureen bristled. She was even more annoyed by what she considered media attempts to misrepresent her feminism. In her eyes, journalists took her assertion that she was a feminist and twisted it to imply that she was against such so-called feminine qualities as sensitivity and concern for others.

For a while on May 22, 1979, however, none of it seemed to matter. On that day, Joe became prime minister, and Maureen was totally exhilarated. By and large, she enjoyed the months they spent at 24 Sussex Drive. There were, of course, a few episodes that caused her perturbation.

One occurred about a week after they had moved into the prime minister's official residence. Just after midnight, Maureen decided to go downstairs for a glass of milk. Without turning on the lights, she opened the refrigerator, poured the milk and was just turning to go back to her room when suddenly she was startled by a man's voice demanding to know what she was doing. Dropping the glass, Maureen screamed to alert the Mounties on patrol outside, then groped frantically for a knife. Within seconds, Joe and two live-in maids came rushing to her rescue. As it turned out, the man was a security officer assigned, without Maureen's knowledge, to patrol the main floor of the house from midnight until 6 a.m.

Another time, at Harrington Lake, she was out alone in a canoe when a summer storm blew up. Paddling to the safety of a small island, she worried that someone would be injured trying to find her. After waiting out the storm, she returned to the dock and was, as she later described it, "humbled" to discover that no one had even missed her. The staff had assumed she was upstairs napping.

In recalling her days at 24 Sussex Drive, Maureen said that it had taken a lot of her time just to attend all the functions she was requested to. She found that most organizers, accustomed to the profile traditionally assumed by prime ministers' wives, did not expect her to comment or to do anything that required thought. They just wanted her to look good and be there.

For a woman of Maureen's dynamic nature, it was clearly not enough. Fortunately, her political interests provided an outlet for her energy. (Margaret Trudeau once commented that the very fact Maureen is so politically attuned keeps her sane.) As her list of both public and private duties grew, it became obvious that Maureen needed help. Eventually, the Conservative Party assigned her a secretary. Mila Mulroney, who in 1984 was given not only a secretary but also an executive assistant, an administrative assistant and an office, acknowledged that Maureen had made it easier for other prime ministers' wives by becoming so involved. According to Mila, the ground work laid by Maureen has ensured that no one now questions the right of the prime minister's wife to have her own staff and to lead her own life.

When the Conservative government fell in 1979 and Maureen returned to Stornoway, she revealed that, despite her staunch feminism, there had been times during Joe's brief term of office when she had been intimidated by a man. The chef at 24 Sussex Drive ruled the kitchen with an iron hand, and Maureen believed that she had made a mistake by allowing him to make her feel like an intruder every time she went to check on a meal. On hot summer nights, she had yearned for barbecued steak but had eaten whatever was placed before her just to preserve harmony below stairs. Only at Harrington Lake had she been able to run her own kitchen and cook the Italian dishes she loved. There, in the rambling, farm-style kitchen, she had gained a perspective on the life she was then living. Once, when a male Tory traditionalist expressed surprise that a woman of Maureen's feminist principles enjoyed cooking, Maureen replied: "Well, you know, we libbers have to eat too!"

After the defeat of the government, Maureen again hit the campaign trail. Putting her dislike of flying behind her, she crisscrossed the country, talking to voters and informing them of her husband's efforts to promote sexual equality by appointing women to both Cabinet and senior advisory positions. During what little time she had for herself, she pored over law books. Her legal career had been on hold long enough, and she wanted to pass her bar exams as quickly as possible.

Eventually, the strain began to show. In Winnipeg, a high-school student asked Maureen why she had kept her maiden name. It was a question that had been asked a hundred times. All at once, however, Maureen found the frustration too much. Her voice cracked and tears rolled down her cheeks.

It became clear, not long after, that the Conservatives were fighting a losing battle. Not even Maureen's determination could return Joe's government to power, and on February 18, 1980, the Liberals, under Pierre Trudeau, were swept to victory. Shocked and angry, Maureen needed time to sort out her feelings. She soon realized that she had to make a life for herself outside politics and later that year earned admission to the Ontario bar.

Unfortunately, political pressure prevented her from going into practice. For the next three years she and Joe fought to stem growing dissatisfaction among rank and file Conservatives with his leadership of the Party. To make matters worse, Maureen's high political profile created other difficulties. As Geills Turner said, one of the greatest problems was the inability of the public to accept the fact that Maureen had changed the traditionally supportive role of a politician's wife into a full partnership. All people could see was that Maureen had influence, and they were concerned that she and the wives of other M.P.s would one day become involved in policy decisions.

Maureen listened to it all. If the criticism wore her down, she tried not to show it. After the election, she turned to her other great interest: writing. With characteristic gusto, she began researching a book on the official homes of the prime minister and the leader of the Opposition. The book, *Residences*, became a national best seller and quickly sold more than thirty thousand copies.

When a Progressive Conservative leadership convention was held in 1983, Maureen returned once more to the hustings. Addressing youth rallies and women's groups and appearing frequently in Quebec, she worked tirelessly to win support for her husband. As a result, Joe had most of the women and youth delegates in his camp when voting began, as well as half the delegates from Quebec. But it was not enough. Standing together on the stage after the results of the final ballot had been announced, dignified in defeat, Maureen and Joe congratulated the new leader, Brian Mulroney. While millions of Canadians watched on television, Maureen clenched her hands and stood rigidly at attention as the national anthem brought the convention to a close. Afterwards, all she wanted was to get away. With Joe and their daughter, Catherine, she left on a five-week trip to Europe.

Although she felt that Joe had been treated shabbily by the party, she determinedly put the past behind her. In demand as a speaker, she told one group after another that women must prepare themselves to take their place in the new high-tech work force. She also spoke on the need for both better pension plans for women and tax breaks for people who volunteer their time to charities.

Eventually, she and Joe bought a three-bedroom stucco house near Parliament Hill. After they had unpacked, Maureen admitted that with all the moves she has made since her marriage, she never settles down in a house without recognizing the fact that one day she will leave it.

If she is practical by nature, she is also true to her feminist principles. In April, 1984, she made it clear that her support of women knows no party bounds. While candidates were declaring their intention of seeking the leadership of the Liberal Party following the resignation of Prime Minister Pierre Trudeau, Maureen said she thought it would be "healthy for the system" if Liberal Party president Iona Campagnolo entered the race. She went on to say that not only could Iona do it, many feminists felt she had a responsibility to do it. The fact that a victory by Campagnolo might encourage Conservative women to support the Liberals in the next election did not seem to sway Maureen's belief that it was vital for a woman to run for prime minister. Unfortunately, not even feminist support could convince Campagnolo to put forward her name, and John Turner succeeded Pierre Trudeau as leader of the Liberal Party and prime minister of Canada.

As it turned out, Turner's term of office was destined to be short. An election was called for September 4, 1984; and during the last days of the campaign, rumors began to circulate that Maureen and Joe were experiencing severe marital problems. Joe's executive assistant felt the gossip started when Joe checked in alone at an Ottawa hotel while furniture was being moved into a new house he and Maureen had bought near Aylmer, a few miles from Ottawa. Maureen, still compaigning for the Conservative Party, was unable to join him. When the reports grew more persistent, she and Joe issued a terse denial; and Maureen later said she believed the story had been started by a journalist.

Following the Conservative victory in September, Joe was named Minister for External Affairs in the Cabinet of Prime Minister Brian Mulroney. In March, 1985, Maureen received an appointment of her own. The Toronto law firm of Lyons, Arbus and Goodman announced that Maureen, with her "wide-ranging perspective on the many legal, economic, and social changes now facing Canada," would open their new office in Ottawa. Although she had done the required articling and had been admitted to the Ontario bar, it marked her debut as a practicing attorney.

Later that year, she accompanied Joe on an eight-day visit to the Soviet Union. Following her own itinerary, she met with Soviet Deputy Premier Lydia Lykova, toured an art museum, talked with law students, and visited a kindergarten. The blatancy of the propaganda she encountered amazed her, and she later said the trip had given her a new appreciation of the freedom she enjoyed in Canada. For the first time, she felt that she had been too blasé in protecting the various aspects of liberty. If her past actions are any indication, she will no doubt draw upon the experience in the years to come as she continues to champion women's rights.

GEILLS TURNER

Geills Turner, wife of Canada's seventeenth prime minister, John Turner, is an avowed perfectionist. Whether pursuing her own academic interests, working out at her weight-training club, or campaigning for her husband, she has one goal: to obtain the best results possible. Yet despite her past achievements in classrooms, athletic centres and meeting halls, Geills is totally self-effacing: "I'm not that confident," she said in 1984. "Confidence is only related to your success."

The daughter of wealthy insurance executive, David Kilgour, Geills was born in Winnipeg in 1938. She inherited her father's quick temper and strong will and from childhood was encouraged to think for herself and to voice her opinions. Over the years, a special bond developed between Geills (a Gaelic name, pronounced "Jill") and her father; and on canoe trips together, Mr. Kilgour taught his only daughter to value fair play, to stand up for her beliefs and never to give in.

As a student at Balmoral Hall, a private girls' school in Winnipeg, Geills did well. She was popular and outgoing, but like Maureen McTeer, valued her privacy. Her competitive — often compulsive — nature manifested itself early, and she found that tennis, basketball and volleyball provided badly needed outlets for tension. Once during her years at Balmoral Hall, she won the Manitoba gymnastics competition and in her final term was appointed school sports captain.

At the University of Manitoba, she studied mathematics. One classmate remembers her as the only woman capable enough to be asked to do problems at the

Geills Turner

blackboard. Two years later, Geills moved on to McGill University in Montreal. Graduating in 1959 with a degree in mathematics and physics, she enrolled in a business administration course at Harvard University. The following year she went to New York and worked for IBM designing computer programs for important corporate clients.

In 1962, she returned to Montreal where John Turner, a young Liberal she had met through mutual friends while attending McGill, asked her to work on his campaign for the federal riding of St. Lawrence-St. George. Collaborating with another computer programmer, Geills set up a system that broke down previous election results poll by poll. Romance blossomed amid the strewn printout sheets; and on May 11, 1963, the math whiz married the new member of St. Lawrence-St. George.

As Geills later said, married women who *could* stay home in the 1960s, *did*; and she was no exception. Although she missed the challenge of the business world at first, she has no regrets about her decision to withdraw from the work force. In her opinion, two careers infringe on the time mothers have to spend with their children.

Political life was new for Geills; and to protect her privacy, she cultivated a small circle of friends who helped her maintain a low profile by refusing to discuss her with outsiders. Yet even among the members of her loyal coterie, Geills became noted for her acerbic comments. Brought up to have a mind of her own, she is not a woman to keep quiet about things that displease her. Her own awareness of her sharp tongue encouraged her for years to stay away from the media so that exaggerated accounts of her remarks would not affect her husband's career.

When John decided to run for the leadership of the Liberal Party in 1968, Geills worked diligently on his campaign. After his defeat, however, she withdrew more deeply behind her wall of privacy; and despite the attention John received as federal finance minister, she refused to be drawn before the public eye.

In December, 1971, she invited Pierre and Margaret Trudeau to Christmas dinner. Geills knew that Margaret, who was expecting her first baby on December 25, would not be able to fly home to Vancouver for the holidays and thought that she and Pierre would enjoy being with other people. To Geills' surprise, Margaret declined, saying that she would be spending Christmas Day in the delivery room. Geills urged her to reconsider and pointed out that babies rarely arrive on the date they are due. Margaret remained firm, however, and on December 25 gave birth to a son. In 1984 Geills said that she admired Margaret and felt that she had had a "tough" time trying to figure out what her role as wife of the prime minister really was.

During John's years in the federal Cabinet, Geills accompanied him on business trips whenever she could. Not only does she enjoy travelling, she enjoys being with John and feels that it is important for husbands and wives to be together as often as possible. At home, she gives family life a high priority and has established a rule that everyone be home for Sunday dinner.

Yet in the early 1970s, not even her happy home life completely satisfied Geills. She needed something more and for a time while John held the finance portfolio considered working toward a degree in law. It would have meant attending university full time, however; and in the end, she decided it would not be fair to her four children.

Then, in 1976, John resigned from politics and accepted a partnership in a Toronto law firm. The time was finally right for Geills to reestablish her own identity. With her youngest child ready for school, she enrolled in a four-year photography course at Ryerson Polytechnical Institute. She recalls that for the first few weeks she felt quite threatened. Studying with strangers half her age unsettled her, and it was not until her competitive instincts kicked into gear that she finally settled down. Although she found the course demanding, it was important to her to discover that she could still function as an individual. One thing she could not do, was lessen her desire for privacy. During her years at Ryerson, she refused to show pictures of her family's Christmas celebrations even to her photography instructor.

Eventually a threat to the security of her life away from the public eye *did* develop. Pierre Trudeau resigned from office late in November, 1979; and for a time, John considered running for the Liberal leadership. Geills was not eager to see her husband return to politics and must have felt relieved when Trudeau withdrew his resignation and John continued with his law practice. Four and a half years later, Trudeau stepped down again — this time for good — and John reconsidered seeking the leadership. Alone on a beach in Jamaica, he and Geills agreed the time was right. The children were older and it would probably be John's last chance.

For most of the three-month campaign that followed, Geills kept out of public view. She left on a skiing holiday with the children after she and John returned from Jamaica and was in China on a twenty-day photography tour when the Liberals began choosing convention delegates. Then, as the leadership race entered its last three weeks, she went to work. Accompanying John on his cross-country travels, she reacclimatized herself to politics by attending rallies and meeting delegates. Although she had hoped to maintain what she called a private position, she admitted that it was impossible; and after sixteen years of refusing to grant interviews, she gave four in one day. She replied graciously and often at length to questions about her favorite subjects — sports, travel and photography — but steadfastly refused to discuss her personal life.

Once she became more comfortable at Liberal gatherings, she decided to strike out on her own. With characteristic determination, she addressed gatherings in New Brunswick, Manitoba, Quebec and the Northwest Territories. In her first public speech since running for the executive of the Women's Athletic Association of McGill University in 1959, she showed her social consciousness and impressed a group of working mothers in Sackville, N.B. by suggesting that empty churches and schools be put to use as day-care centers.

The experience drained her, but she soon looked upon campaigning as a job. One friend, commenting on the threat campaigning posed to Geills' way of life, said she believed that Geills had hit the hustings becamse her competitive instinct was stronger than even her need for privacy. Another said that seeing John lose would be the hardest part of all for Geills. As it turned out, the Turner camp did not have to worry about defeat — at least not during the leadership convention. John won on the second ballot.

In the weeks that followed, Geills had little time to enjoy her role as wife of Canada's seventeenth prime minister. Although she wanted to familiarize herself with the problems of less-privileged women in order to focus government attention on them, she found herself spending most of her time addressing crowds and talking to reporters. John had called an election for September 4, and it was clear the Liberals were in trouble.

As the campaign heated up, Geills concentrated on social issues. She decided to say what she thought and to forget about her sharp tongue. After two weeks of travelling with John, she headed out on her own. In Swift Current, she accused the Conservatives of becoming Liberals overnight and said that many of the policies put forward by the Conservatives bore a striking resemblance to those proposed by the Liberals. She then turned her sights on the New Democratic Party and suggested that Ed Broadbent was only offering extravagant promises on women's issues because he knew he would not form the next government. John could not make similar promises, she explained, because "he has to be fiscally responsible and be able to put into effect the things he promises because he is a man of his word."

Clearly, her remarks were partisan; but she proved five days later that she said what she thought and not what Liberal strategists told her to say. In Simcoe, Ontario she stood up against the Liberal government's defense policy by announcing her support of a nuclear freeze. "Every serious, intelligent human being would be in favor of a freeze . . ." she said, "because what we're talking about is the potential annihilation of the entire race." (Just a few days earlier, John had issued a policy paper that said Canada would pursue peace initiatives while adhering to NATO policy, which does *not* endorse a freeze on nuclear arms production.) When reporters asked Geills if John had been aware of the contents of her speech, she said: "No, I don't think so. He has confidence in me. Whether it's well-placed or not remains to be seen."

Geills also has confidence in John: but it did not prevent her from stating her belief that the prime minister's wife has both a right and a responsibility to influence her husband privately on important issues. "There may be lots of

163

husbands who don't talk to their wives at all," she said. "In a general, philosophical way, I can influence my husband. It depends on what I'm talking about." Although she said she would be uncomfortable disagreeing with John in public, she admitted that she would never back down unless she was convinced she was wrong. She feels striking a balance between feelings and good judgment is important. When one journalist asked if she felt she was abusing her privileged access to the prime minister, she replied tartly: "I find that a ridiculous question."

Reports after the election suggested that Geills, John's press aide and tour director had argued frequently during the campaign over who was in charge and that John's campaign chief had asked Geills to campaign by herself and to stay off the main campaign airplane. Regardless of whatever friction existed, Geills remained aggressive and outspoken. Two days before the election, she spoke with an anti-cruise protester saying: "Let's hope that Reagan isn't reelected." Although she refused to sign the peace petition the man held out to her, she urged him to carry his mission to the United States. "I think the American people feel strongly about this, too," she said, "and Reagan is coming out with a kind of escalation."

Before the campaign had even started, a friend suggested that Geills was uncomfortable keeping quiet. By the time it was winding down, Geills admitted that she had wanted to do more than stand beside her husband smiling, receiving flowers, and being what she called "a sort of adornment on the stage." Clearly, she had achieved her objective; but despite her best efforts, the Liberals were doomed. When the final results were in, the Liberals had been soundly defeated; and John, after a mere ten weeks in power, was replaced by Brian Mulroney.

Geills returned to their home in Toronto and prepared for the move to Stornoway, the home of the leader of the Opposition. Although her new role places demands on her time, it does not require her to be constantly in the public eye. Many Liberal supporters believe, however, that the greater Geills' visibility, the greater the party's chances for reelection. They see her as an excellent ambassador for the Liberal cause, and one suggested during the 1984 election campaign that

Geills might eventually be an ideal candidate for prime minister. "You know," he said, "I'd run her against Maureen McTeer any day."

MILA MULRONEY

Combining the sophistication of Jacqueline Kennedy with the warmth of the Queen Mother, Mila Mulroney is probably the most popular prime minister's wife in Canadian history. Crowds flock to see her wherever she goes; and in the spring of 1985, Conservative polls indicated that she was even more highly regarded than her husband, who, at the time, had a leadership approval rating of between eighty-three and eighty-nine per cent.

Certainly there was nothing in Mila's early life to suggest that she was destined for celebrity status. Born in Sarajevo, Yugoslavia on July 15, 1953, she immigrated to Canada with her parents at the age of five. Her father, Dimitrije Pivnicki, a physician, saw little future for his family under the postwar communist regime and decided to make a new start in Montreal.

Although the Pivnickis spent their first years in Canada in a modest apartment, they managed to send their only daughter to a private girls' elementary school. Mila, a student of average ability, went on to Westmount High School and later enrolled at Sir George Williams University (now Concordia) in Montreal.

Then, in 1972, she met Brian Mulroney, a thirty-three-year-old lawyer from Baie Comeau, Quebec. As Mila remembers it, she was sitting by the pool at the Mount Royal Tennis Club in Montreal eating a tomato sandwich when Brian walked up to her. She did not consider him particularly good-looking, but she *did* find him interesting and was intrigued

Mila Mulroney

when he began telling her about his prime ministerial ambitions.

Brian's version of their first meeting is somewhat different. Although he agrees that it took place at the Mount Royal Tennis Club, he says he was sitting by the pool reading *The New York Times* when Mila walked by in a bikini and captured his attention. After talking with her and discovering her offhand humor and outgoing personality, he decided he wanted to get to know her better.

They were married within a year. A daughter, Caroline, born in 1974, was followed by sons Benedict in 1976 and Mark in 1979. While pregnant with her second child, Mila left university three credits short of a degree in civil engineering. She has no regrets: as a young girl she used to tell her parents that her one ambition was to be a mother. When pushed further about her decision to abandon her education, she explains that it was *her* choice and that she never looks back.

When Brian ran unsuccessfully for the leadership of the Conservative Party in 1976, Mila, then well advanced in her second pregnancy, did little more than smile for the cameras. In the rocky days following her husband's defeat, she refused to allow herself to become depressed. Her formula for dealing with setbacks is to have a good cry, then forget about them.

Although close friends insist that Mila played a key role in helping Brian give up alcohol in the years after the Tory convention, Mila refuses to admit it. "I never thought it was my business," she insists. "We don't tread on each other's turf."

When Brian reoffered for the Conservative leadership in 1983, Mila emerged as a valuable vote gatherer. Her children were old enough to be left behind, and she wanted to do what she could to help Brian achieve his goal. On the campaign trail, her mixture of warmth, sophistication, and little-girl charm endeared her to delegates. In the end, Brian won the leadership but Mila's job was far from over.

During her husband's first year as leader of the Opposition, she received more than fifteen hundred requests to make personal appearances. Even when she was home at Stornoway her time was not her own. After moving into the official residence of the leader of the Opposition on December

5, 1983, she and Brian held their first party on the 6th and by the 20th had hosted eight more. In fifteen days, Mila had greeted twenty-five hundred guests.

The following year her schedule became even more hectic. An election was called for September 4, and Conservative organizers immediately made it clear they considered Mila a major political asset to both her husband and the party. They included her in most of Brian's campaign trips and featured her prominently in party advertising. With Mila's vivacity and Brian's ebullience, the Conservatives had something Canadians responded to — a charismatic couple that bore a striking similarity to John and Jacqueline Kennedy.

Although Mila seldom made speeches or held press conferences during the campaign, she told one group in Montreal: "I live by one overriding principle — my partnership with Brian comes first." A year later she told an American audience that her role as "maintainer of the [family] status quo" and her desire to support her husband had "already earned me the reputation of being a traditional wife. I am not sure that comment is offered as a compliment."

It was *not*. Feminists took exception to what some called her "happy homemaker" remarks and castigated her for being content to live a protected and privileged life. Other women criticized her for her fondness of expensive clothes and for her habit of flying from Ottawa to Montreal every three weeks to have her bangs trimmed by her favorite hair stylist. But while some women berated her, thousands more envied her the security and affluence she enjoyed as the wife of a prosperous politician. Mila is keenly aware of the way others view her, but she makes no apologies for enjoying the good things of life.

As the campaign gained momentum, she silenced some of her critics and drew applause from many of her supporters by calling for more women to become involved in politics. "We have three women in the House of Commons now," she said, "and those three women are all remarkable. But we need many more.... I've had a chance to talk to a lot of women across Canada and we're unanimous — we all want our children's well-being, [and] we want jobs . . ." She said she would like to

169

see a dozen women elected to the House of Commons because they would debate from a woman's point of view and perhaps bring about changes in government policy. She refused to speculate, however, on whether women would be considered for Cabinet positions. Decisions of that nature, she insisted, would be made by her husband.

As the weeks passed, her popularity grew; and despite the crowds that pressed around her wherever she went, Mila seemed to enjoy herself. "People who grab for you, vote for you," she laughed. Conservative Party organizers were delighted by her success.

There were, of course, negative aspects to her new celebrity status. She had little time to spend with her children, and the stress and long hours wore her down. But Mila refused to complain. Instead, she concentrated on the positive side of it all — the greater closeness she enjoyed with her husband.

When Brian was elected with a large majority on September 4, Mila was euphoric. Together they went to work in the Prime Minister's Office, a large suite in the Langevin Building on Parliament Hill. For the first time in Canadian history, the prime minister's wife had her own office and a staff of three. When controversy arose over the necessity for such support, Mila declared simply that if she didn't need it, she wouldn't have it. She estimated in 1985 that she receives between thirty and fifty letters a week as well as scores of telephone calls requesting her to do everything from attend community bazaars to intervene at immigration hearings.

As far as official entertaining is concerned, Mila has not evinced the same enthusiasm as wife of the prime minister that she did as wife of the leader of the Opposition. "There's not going to be gay laughter and entertaining at 24 [Sussex Drive]," she said in an interview on the CTV public affairs program, "W-5", "until a lot of people are put back to work . . . I think that the Canadian people would not want their prime minister entertaining until the opportunity that this country is famous for is returned." She has been true to her word: between September, 1984 and May, 1985, she and Brian hosted only two modest parties.

During the first months her husband held office, Mila rarely discussed political issues in public. She said she did not feel she should become involved in things she knew nothing about and added that Brian's job was none of her business. The only subjects she would speak about were those she was familiar with — such as projects to help handicapped children and the disadvantaged.

As her self-assurance grew, however, Mila became more vocal. When Health and Welfare Minister Jake Epp announced in the spring of 1985 that medical research funding would be increased to $158 million a year from $125 million, instead of being reduced as had been expected, a Mulroney aide admitted that the additional funding had been made available after private lobbying by Mila.

People who had expected the new prime minister's wife to be a mere ribbon cutter and sod turner were surprised by her decision to become involved in public affairs. For Mila, there was nothing surprising about the decision at all. Although she had been uncomfortable addressing her first few audiences during the election campaign, she had gradually grown accustomed to it and by September 4 was actually enjoying it. As she later said, she likes being tested.

When Dinah Shore offered to donate $25,000 to Mila's favorite charity if she would be guest speaker at the annual Dinah Shore Golf Classic in Palm Springs, Florida, Mila accepted. With her increased confidence, she was able to let her effervescent charm and roguish good humor come to the fore. "For all that money," she quipped, "I could get to like this!"

During an interview she gave in Washington, D.C., in April, 1985, Mila made it clear that her reticence about discussing politics in public was gone. "If there are issues I . . . feel strongly about, I'm obviously going to be vocal about them." She had earlier given a glimpse of her new assertiveness by attacking the former Liberal government. "Brian and his Cabinet . . .," she said, "didn't inherit a very pretty picture. The financial cupboard was bare."

Usually, however, she has stuck to non-political subjects. At a fund-raising dinner held by the Canadian Cystic Fibrosis Foundation in the spring of 1985, she delighted guests by revealing that the initial draft of her speech, prepared by her husband's aides, had not quite measured up to her standards.

"I do appreciate," she said, "that Canada is a country of small towns and big dreams, but I didn't feel quite comfortable saying that — so I went on to [write my own] draft number two." Pausing for just a moment, she threw her arms up in the air. "I had no option," she grinned, "the devil made me do it."

As honorary chairperson of the Canadian Cystic Fibrosis Foundation, Mila is not content merely to appear at galas and to lend her name. When she agreed to work for the organization, she insisted upon being thoroughly briefed on both the disease and ongoing research so that she could speak authoritatively.

Her conscientiousness manifested itself again at a first ladies' summit on drug abuse held in Washington, D.C. in April, 1985. Mila impressed members of the media by her insightful comments and by the fact that she was one of the few delegates to listen attentively to the many lengthy speeches. Her interest was genuine, and her knowledge of the subject was the result of several meetings with representatives of the Department of Health and Welfare. Before she left for Ottawa, she was front-page news: reporters wanted to know everything about her — from her background to her shoe size.

In Britain a month later on her last major trip before the birth of her fourth child, she attracted even greater coverage and so inspired one writer for the London *Daily Express* that he called her "the most glamorous political star since the early Jackie Kennedy."

For the most part, Mila enjoys her role as wife of the prime minister. "I accept the terms and conditions that go with it," she said in 1985. "In all honesty, I have no problems." Her positive approach helps her cope with the lack of privacy and with the frustration of not knowing what people expect of her until after the fact. It also influences her philosophy on child rearing. She has a rule: her children must never say " can't." Mila wants them to believe as she does that everything is possible.

BIBLIOGRAPHY

Aberdeen, Lady. *The Canadian Journal of Lady Aberdeen 1893-1898.* Toronto: The Champlain Society, 1960.

Aberdeen, Lord and Lady. *We Twa.* 2 vols. London: W. Collins Sons & Co. Ltd., 1926.

Armstrong, Sally. "Mila One Year Later," *Canadian Living,* August, 1985, p. 88-94.

Bannerman, Jean. *Leading Ladies.* Dundas, Ont.: Carrswood, 1967.

Berton, Pierre. "I Spend Election Night with Mr. and Mrs. Pearson," *Maclean's,* May 4, 1963, p. 60.

Borden, Robert Laird. *Letters to Limbo.* ed. Henry Borden. Toronto: University of Toronto Press, 1971.

-----. *Robert Laird Borden: His Memoirs.* 2 vols. ed. Heath Macquarrie. Toronto: McClelland & Stewart Limited, 1969.

Bothwell, Robert. *Pearson: His Life and World.* Toronto: McGraw-Hill Ryerson Ltd., 1978.

Brown, Robert Craig. *Robert Laird Borden.* vol. I. Toronto: The Macmillan Company of Canada Limited, 1975.

-----. *Robert Laird Borden.* vol. II. Toronto: Macmillan of Canada, 1980.

Buckingham, William, and G.W. Ross. *The Honorable Alexander Mackenzie: His Life and Times.* Toronto: Rose Publishing Company (Limited), 1892.

Cahill, Jack. *John Turner: The Long Run.* Toronto: McClelland & Steward Limited, 1984.

Callwood, June. *The Naughty Nineties.* Toronto: NSL Natural Science of Canada Limited, 1977.

Cameron, Stevie. "Maggie: Happy at Last!" *Chatelaine,* June, 1985, p. 56-57, 106-110.

-----. "The New Political Wives," *Chatelaine*, December, 1984, p. 60-61, 136-142.

Clippingdale, Richard. *Laurier: His Life and World.* Toronto: McGraw-Hill Ryerson Limited, 1979.

Cochrane, Felicity. *Margaret Trudeau: The Prime Minister's Runaway Wife.* Scarborough, Ont.: The New American Library of Canada, Limited, 1978.

Collard, Edgar A. *Canadian Yesterdays.* Toronto: Longmans, Green and Company, 1955.

Creighton, Donald. *John A. Macdonald: The Young Politician.* Toronto: The Macmillan Company of Canada Limited, 1965.

Diefenbaker, John G. *One Canada: Memoirs of the Right Honorable John G. Diefenbaker. Volume I 1895-1956.* Toronto: The Macmillan Company of Canada Limited, 1975.

-----. *One Canada: Memoirs of the Right Honorable John G. Diefenbaker. Volume 2 1956-1962.* Toronto: The Macmillan Company of Canada Limited, 1976.

-----. *One Canada: Memoirs of the Right Honorable John G. Diefenbaker. Volume 3 1962-1967.* Toronto: The Macmillan Company of Canada Limited, 1977.

Dilschneider, Donna. "What Mrs. Pearson Really Thinks," *The Canadian*, March, 1967, p. 3-6.

Donaldson, Gordon. *Sixteen Men.* Toronto: Doubleday Canada Limited, 1980.

English, John. *Arthur Meighen.* Don Mills, Ont.: Fitzhenry & Whiteside Limited, 1977.

-----. *Borden: His Life and World.* Toronto: McGraw-Hill Ryerson Limited, 1977.

Graham, Roger. *Arthur Meighen.* vol. I. Toronto: Clarke, Irwin & Company Limited, 1960.

-----. *Arthur Meighen.* vol. II. Toronto: Clarke, Irwin & Company Limited, 1963.

-----. *Arthur Meighen.* vol. III. Toronto: Clarke, Irwin & Company Limited, 1965.

Gray, Charlotte. "Chatelaine's Woman of the Year 1984: Maureen McTeer," *Chatelaine*, January, 1984, p. 52, 120-122, 128-134.

Gwyn, Richard. *The Northern Magus.* Toronto: McClelland & Stewart Limited, 1980.

Gwynn, Sandra. *The Private Capital.* Toronto: McClelland & Stewart Limited, 1984.

Harkin, William (editor). *Political Reminiscences of Sir Charles Tupper, Bart.* London: Constable & Company, Limited, 1914.

Holt, Simma. *The Other Mrs. Diefenbaker.* Markham, Ont.: PaperJacks Ltd., 1984.

Hopkins, J. Castell. *Life and Work of the Rt. Hon. Sir John Thompson.* Brantford, Ont.: Bradley, Garretson & Co., 1895.

-----. *The Canadian Review of Public Affairs 1912.* Toronto: The Annual Review Publishing Company Limited, 1913.

Johnson, J.K. and Carole B. Stelmack (eds.) *The Letters of Sir John A. Macdonald 1858-1861.* vol. II. Ottawa: Public Archives of Canada, 1969.

Longley, J.W. *Sir Charles Tupper.* Toronto: Oxford University Press, 1926.

MacGregor, Roy. "The Politics of Being Nice," *Maclean's*, May 6, 1985, p. 12-14.

McTeer, Maureen. *Residences.* Scarborough, Ont.: Prentice-Hall Canada Inc., 1982.

Morgan, H.J. *Types of Canadian Women.* Toronto: William Briggs, 1903.

Newman, C.M. "Mrs. Lester Pearson's New Life in the Limelight," *Maclean's*, May 7, 1964, p. 26-28, 30-32.

Pearson, Lester B. *Mike: The Memoirs of the Rt. Hon. Lester B. Pearson. vol. I, 1897-1948.* Toronto: University of Toronto Press, 1972.

-----. *Mike: The Memoirs of the Rt. Hon. Lester B. Pearson. vol. II. 1948-1957.* Toronto: University of Toronto Press, 1973.

-----. *Mike: The Memoirs of the Rt. Hon. Lester B. Pearson. vol. III. 1957-1968.* Toronto: University of Toronto Press, 1975.

Phillips, Alan. "Olive Diefenbaker's Not-so-private Life," *Maclean's*, December 21, 1957, p. 18-19, 53-54.

Pickersgill, J.W. *Louis St. Laurent.* Don Mills, Ont.: Fitzhenry & Whiteside Limited, 1981.

-----. *My Years with Louis St. Laurent.* Toronto: University of Toronto Press, 1975.

Radwanski, George. *Trudeau.* Scarborough, Ont.: The New American Library of Canada, Limited, 1979.

Reynolds, Louise. *Agnes: The Biography of Lady Macdonald.* Toronto: Samuel-Stevens, Publishers, Ltd., 1979.

Saunders, Kathleen. *Robert Borden.* Don Mills, Ont.: Fitzhenry & Whiteside Limited, 1978.

Schull, Joseph. *Laurier: The First Canadian.* Toronto: Macmillan of Canada, 1965.

Skelton, Oscar. *Life and Letters of Sir Wilfrid Laurier.* vol. I. Toronto: Oxford University Press, 1921.

-----. *Life and Letters of Sir Wilfrid Laurier.* vol. II, New York: The Century Co., 1922.

Spencer, Arthur. "How Mrs. Mike Sees Diplomatic Ottawa," *Mayfair*, October, 1952, p. 46-47, 95, 97-99.

Spigelman, Martin. *Wilfrid Laurier.* Don Mills, Ont.: Fitzhenry & Whiteside Limited, 1978.

Swainson, Donald. *Macdonald of Kingston.* Toronto: Personal Library, 1979.

Thomson, Dale C. *Alexander Mackenzie: Clear Grit.* Toronto: The Macmillan Company of Canada, Limited, 1960.

-----. *Louis St. Laurent: Canadian.* Toronto: Macmillan of Canada, 1967.

Thordarson, Bruce. *Lester Pearson: Diplomat and Politician.* Toronto: Oxford University Press, 1974.

Trudeau, Margaret. *Beyond Reason.* Markham, Ont.: Paperjacks Ltd., 1980.

Tupper, Charles. *Recollections of Sixty Years.* London: Cassell and Company, Ltd., 1914.

Tupper, Charles Hibbert. *Supplement to the Life and Letters of the Rt. Hon. Sir Charles Tupper, Bart., G.C.M.G.* Toronto: The Ryerson Press, 1926.

Turcotte, Eileen and John Kingston. "PMs' Wives: How Does Margaret Fit The Mold?" *Chatelaine*, December, 1971, p. 22-23, 38-42.

Waite, P.B. *Macdonald: His Life and World.* Toronto: McGraw-Hill Ryerson Limited, 1975.

Woods, Shirley, E. *Ottawa: The Capital of Canada.* Toronto: Doubleday Canada Limited, 1980.

Newspapers

The Amherst Daily News
The Halifax Chronicle
The Moncton Times
The Ottawa Citizen
The Toronto Globe and Mail

Various dates were consulted from all of the above (1867-1985).

Collections of Private Papers

Borden, Sir Robert L., Papers. Public Archives of Canada.

Macdonald, Sir John A., Papers. Public Archives of Canada.

Mackenzie, Alexander, Papers. Public Archives of Canada.

Thompson, Sir John, Papers. Public Archives of Canada.

Tupper, Sir Charles, Papers. Public Archives of Nova Scotia.

THE AUTHOR

Carol McLeod was born in Halifax, Nova Scotia. In 1970, after studies at Mount Allison University, she joined the staff of the *Amherst Daily News.* One year later she joined the Canadian Imperial Bank of Commerce. In 1979 Mrs. McLeod resigned her position to devote her time to free-lance writing. Her work has been accepted by a number of Canadian and American publications. She is author of *Legendary Canadian Women* (1983) and *Glimpses into New Brunswick History* (1984), both published by Lancelot Press. Mrs. McLeod presently lives in Moncton, New Brunswick, with her husband David.